AWAKEN
— AND —
RISE

BRIAN LIDLE

The Brian Lidle Company
www.brianlidle.com
thebrianlidlecompany@gmail.com

Author and Speaker
Contact Brian to speak and inspire at your next event

Copyright © 2017 Brian Lidle

All rights reserved. No part of this publication may be reproduced, stored in any retrieval system, distributed, or transmitted in any form or by any means, including photocopying, recording, or other electronic or mechanical methods, without the prior written permission of the author/publisher, except in the case of brief quotations embodied in critical reviews and certain other noncommercial uses permitted by copyright law.

For permission requests, write to the publisher, addressed "Attention: Permissions Coordinator," at the address below.

thebrianlidlecompany@gmail.com

Cover Design by Jennifer Deese
Interior Design by Jennifer Deese
Proofreading/Editing by Jennifer Deese
Cover Photo by Netfalls Remy Musser via Shutterstock

Ordering Information:
Available for purchase on Amazon.com

ISBN 978-0-9986775-0-7 (Paperback)
ISBN 978-0-9986775-1-4 (eBook)

Library of Congress Control Number: 2017902724
Brian Lidle Company, The, Hilliard, Ohio

This is a work of fiction. Names, characters, businesses, places, events and incidents are either the products of the author's imagination or used in a fictitious manner. Any resemblance to actual persons, living or dead, or actual events is purely coincidental.

Limit of Liability/Disclaimer of Warranty: While the publisher and author have used their best efforts in preparing this book, they make no representations or warranties with respect to the accuracy or completeness of the contents of this book and specifically disclaim any implied warranties of merchantability or fitness for a particular purpose. No warranty may be created or extended by sales representatives or written sales materials.
The advice and strategies contained therein may not be suitable for your situation. You should consult with a professional where appropriate. Neither the publisher nor author shall be liable for any loss of profit or any other commercial damages, including but not limited to special, incidental, consequential, or other damages.

Printed in the United States of America

THE GUIDE TO
R.I.S.E.

After reading **Awaken and Rise**, you may find yourself wondering if there is something more. You may be wondering about your gifts and purpose.

The Guide to R.I.S.E. was created with you in mind. This guide takes you through a process similar to John's journey to find your gifts and purpose. This helpful process can be found at our website along with other content intended to inspire and motivate you to go for your dreams.

Find it at BrianLidle.com

"Our greatest glory is not in never falling, but in RISING every time we fall."

To the love of my life, Michele, without your love and support,
my dream would be unfulfilled.

To my parents, Bob and Talli, who never wanted me to
be anything other than me.

To Chloe, Sophia, and Gavin, never compromise who you are, for
you are enough. You are powerful being uniquely you.

II

AUTHOR'S NOTE

Thank you for purchasing Awaken and Rise. In these pages, you will find my heart, soul, and the valuable lessons that served to inspire me to live a life true to myself. Initially, I set out to write as an expression of creativity, but as I grew, my soul cried out to share a story that would serve to inspire and empower you.

In a world that is constantly trying to measure, compare, and elevate certain aspects of one person over another, we have lost the knowledge of how uniquely powerful and gifted each of us are. We have become distracted by the need to achieve, accomplish, and establish a reputation because of the unwritten and constrictive rules of society. These rules are limitations based on the superficial, the material, and the visible; they have no capacity to value and measure the unique potential within you.

Thus you, the individual, supersede those rules! You are only bound to them if you agree to them. If you reject the limitations of what the world says you can be or can do, you will begin to embrace the power you have within.

If you take a look at the lives of several difference-makers, you will see instances of where the world attempted to limit them. Beethoven's music teacher believed he was hopeless. Einstein was considered unintelligent because he couldn't talk until he was four. Winston Churchill failed the sixth grade. Steve Jobs dropped out of college. Oprah Winfrey was fired from her news anchor job. Walt Disney was told he wasn't creative enough. The list goes on and on, but it serves as proof: we are the architects of our lives. We are unique and powerful, especially when the world can't see it.

As you read Awaken and Rise, know that this serves as an homage to the strength, beauty, and unique power you have within to make a difference for our world. Yes, you may struggle, fall, and experience setbacks, but as Confucius said, "Our greatest glory is not in never falling, but in RISING every time we fall." Get back up and refuse to be denied your dreams.

Sincerely,
Brian
Awaken and Rise

TABLE OF CONTENTS

Prologue	1
Introduction	3
1 - The Chance	9
2 - Fear and Stifling	19
3 - Drifting Asleep	25
4 - The Rock	31
5 - The Legacy Awaits	43
6 - The Grind	51
7 - Surrogates	59
8 - Elevation and Despair	63
9 - Success, Discontent, Emptiness, and Legacy	69
10 - A Quick Run	79
11 - Recalibrate	87
12 - Kindness	97
13 - Four Men Discuss	103
14 - Coming Home	107
15 - Inspire	109
16 - Awaken	115
17 - The Sherpa	125

18 - Seek	131
19 - Engage	139
20 - The Power Differential	145
21 - Into Focus	153
22 - Rise	159
23 - We Meet Again	165
24 - The King of Pain	173
25 - Mondays with Mack	179
26 - The Results Are In	187
27 - Not Mutually Exclusive	193
28 - More to Come	203
The Sherpa Playlist	211
Bibliography	214
Acknowledgements	215
About the Author	217

PROLOGUE
THE WORLD BEFORE ME

It was there that he lay face down in the gravel of life. Battered and bloodied with little to show for his impact on the world, he was defeated by the very game that he had mastered. John had no legacy, no memorable history, and no life left within his soul. As John's body functioned only to exist, his soul was feeling the pressure of inconsequence and regret. Energy escaped him and life was hollow. It was then that John started an involuntary quest toward relevance.

As John looked for his soul's source of meaning, he came upon a fire. It warmed him at first and led to comfort, but over time it gained strength and raged. It led to discomfort, challenge, yet it burned away all the distraction and burden that weighed him down. The flames began to consume the old John. They burned all that was false, unnecessary, and vain. As they closed in and ended the life that John thought he wanted, something incredible was happening. He began to gain strength, focus, clarity, and purpose. A second chance emerged as John's soul began to take flight. The flames no longer caused pain, but they turned him into a phoenix. It was this moment when John was conscious of his Awakening and his mission to Rise.

2 AWAKEN AND RISE

INTRODUCTION

So many of us begin with a mindset to make a difference in this world. We focus on being a game changer, someone that matters, and a person who will contribute to the greater good. We normally go into the system of our chosen profession with the idea that we will change things from the inside. Some of us go in audaciously and get smacked around by those who have been there for years. Some of us get conditioned by the system that surrounds us. We find ourselves living out the story of the monkeys, the ladder, and the bananas. There is some debate on whether or not this is true, but either way, it illustrates a very real point.

Seven monkeys are placed into some type of a caged living environment. In the center of this space is a ladder, and at the top of the ladder there are a bunch of bananas. Naturally and immediately a monkey heads towards the ladder. As soon as it touches the ladder, a hose with cold water begins to soak every monkey in the enclosure. This happens over and over again until no monkey goes near the ladder. As time goes on, one of the original monkeys is removed and replaced with a new monkey. After moments of becoming acclimated to the surroundings and new cage mates, the monkey goes for the bananas and touches the ladder. The remaining monkeys attack and teach the lesson that was originally given by the cold water - don't touch the ladder. More time goes by and more original monkeys are replaced by new ones, each suffering a group attack when they head towards the ladder to get the bananas. Eventually, every monkey original to the enclosure is gone from the group. When this happens and the seventh new monkey is introduced, something sad is demonstrated. The seventh monkey heads towards the ladder. Seven is attacked by the other six who have no idea or experience to explain why they are oppressing the seventh's desire to get the bananas. The only explanation is that it has always been done this way – the same justification for many emotions, systems, and processes that we allow to influence our lives today.

This often happens in any profession, system, and life. Many who have been in a static state, whether spending an entire career in one organization, one aspect of a profession, or with one group of people, believe that the dreams of the new are fool-hearted and must be squelched. The battle cry of "we've never done it that way before" echoes through the corridors by different people who directly and indirectly squelch the newcomer's dreams. No one is immune to this conditioning. Great people who have spent their lives and careers following the rules of those in authority or the preferences of their mentors are not immune. They don't want conflict, so they side with the way things were to preserve the relationships they have with other members of the status quo. Usually they don't directly tear anyone or their dreams down, they just don't provide any fuel or positive belief toward these dreams. They conveniently recuse themselves from being a part of the dream. Experience may teach us that they have never been supported to try great things, or they were never led to think and reflect on the "whys" of their life and purpose.

Another person or group of people can be identified as the proverbial negative guard. This group is normally the smallest group in any organization, but 90% of problems and issues seem to arise from this group. The negative guard either despises the new recruits and sabotages their efforts or they work to co-opt their compliance to a perspective that has abandoned hope. They fight against the rays of hope that beam from the hearts of those who want to make a difference. Why? Maybe they were beaten down by others or by their own harsh experiences. Maybe they are struggling with the realities of needing to escape self-condemnation because they abandoned the person they once were, a person who is now a hauntingly distant memory. Maybe they have become miserable people, but usually they have been hurt in one way or another in their personal or professional lives. They have not successfully pushed through to overcome the emotions, self-talk, and persona that hold them far below their potential positive impact.

They fight back with the phrase, "it's always been done this way" or "we tried that once." These phrases can be code for "we are afraid to challenge the status quo," or maybe they once did and failed. The statements can be a quick door out of the conversation to escape the truth that we have been engaged in practices that have governed the way we live, work, and interact, but have never given any real thought. This eliminates personal culpability and responsibility for any damage or inconsideration past practices have caused. The statements can also be said out of laziness. They can be used to push aside that which someone believes is less than important so that they can focus their energies on the urgencies in their immediate world. In the end, that's how the monkeys demonstrate how people oppress each other in any environment. Nevertheless, fear and a scarcity mindset encompass and color thinking, actions, and lives. They hold people back from the beautiful beings they are meant to be.

The third group consists of the true thought and learning leaders. They are transformers to everyone who is impacted by a ripple of their influence. Regardless of the profession or purpose, this group focuses on deep thinking and reflection. They push and want to be pushed in return. They are a rarity in many groups and will go to the wall for anyone trying to take a risk. They will demonstrate loyalty and substance and go all in while demonstrating cautious wisdom. These leaders are often clear on who they are and the purpose they are meant to fulfill. They rise above the distractions around them and see life differently. The learning leaders are the difference-makers and the supporters who enrich the lives of those who listen and learn from their way of living.

This book is about defying the beat-downs and compromises we make in search of our true legacy and purpose. It is all about how we become difference-makers for ourselves and for those we have the opportunity to serve. It holds within it the formula to transition from a state of hollowness and disillusionment to being a member of the transformational group mentioned above.

It is the story of one man who received everything he was told he wanted and became the person he thought he should be. He received all the accolades that come with being at the top of his profession, only to realize it was hollow and unfulfilling. Eventually, it dawned on him that he was living to fulfill the expectations of the world and society. He believed the lies regarding how to be a success and make his life count. He was disillusioned and lost, but when he realized that he had a greater purpose, God and His universe conspired to help him find it.

When we spend a large part of our life invested in the wrong place only to realize the purpose that lies within us, we become powerful advocates for our truth. This book is about what really matters to us: fulfillment, struggle, joy, and purpose.

This is for everyone who has ever realized that there was something more to their life. This is a story about how through the love of God, family, and friends, a person's gifts, passions, and purpose were found, sparking him to AWAKEN and RISE.

8 AWAKEN AND RISE

CHAPTER ONE
THE CHANCE

"Victory!" he thought. Standing at the top of the mountain, achieving all he had set out to accomplish. The world and society promised this would be an amazing and satisfying feeling. John led his team to success and soundly defeated those who stood in the way. He had completed what many believed to be impossible, fulfilled a promise to a friend who had passed away, and proved his own worth to himself, while silencing his doubters. Upon the altar of sacrifice lay John's family, many of his friends, his spirituality, and health. In exchange, John built a legacy of being one of the best in his profession. He had impacted hundreds of lives and his legacy would leave thousands more touched with opportunity beyond their imagination. He stood victorious and hollow.

Several years prior to this moment, John's friend Reuben, who was the superintendent of a large school district, came to him with an opportunity. This wasn't just any opportunity, but THE opportunity that John had been waiting for his entire career: the chance to take on the challenge of a broken and continuously failing school. Its failures were baffling to those inside and outside of the district and community. This school had great students, strong but internally competitive sister schools, and the reputation of being part of an overall top notch organization. Resources were never the problem, but what stunted and sabotaged any potential success was permissive leadership and the self-centered focus of a small group of negative staff members.

Before John's arrival, power struggles were allowed to erupt through passive aggressive methods, and inevitably, the most stubborn and negative personalities won. This caused the many team-focused and student-focused staff members to take a backseat to the needs and wants of the worst teammates. This culture and the results it produced caused concern with stakeholders from every possible group in the organization and throughout the community.

The previous leader, Rex, was a good man who, in John's opinion, lacked the will to take on the difficult issues. Rex was seemingly only willing to work on the positive aspects of the organization. He was a brilliant individual who may have lacked the will needed to renovate and recalibrate the perspectives of that small group of negative people under his supervision. Rex involuntarily allowed the team players to suffer under the will of the selfish. He appreciated his staff, but he never loved his people and students enough to do what made him uncomfortable: being disliked.

Rex may have been tired or distracted, but his focus was elsewhere. After years of cultivating a business relationship with an outside organization, Rex applied for his dream job with them. Reuben was not surprised and genuinely believed Rex would be outstanding in the position. He provided a strong recommendation based on Rex's character and skill set for the job, and Rex's dream job came to fruition and he landed on his feet, right where he was supposed to be. With all of this taking place at an inconvenient time for a school district, there were months of waiting to be done before any departing announcement could take place. However, Reuben was not one to passively wait; he would move behind the scenes to make sure this school had the leader he felt was the right fit. Reuben wanted John to lead.

John recognized that this was his moment. This was the coalescing of all the years of his hard work, taking calculated risks, sacrifice, and learning. Although a master at rolling the dice, he couldn't risk any delay in his response. Reuben posed to John the idea in concept on a Friday night. John couldn't wait the weekend to let Reuben know how excited and interested he was in this opportunity. Since it was a Sunday, Reuben was not in his office, but John left these words for Reuben to be heard on Monday morning: "Reuben, I can't believe it took me 36 hours to call you. I should have told you immediately that I want this opportunity. I promise that I won't fail. Thank you for believing in me and let's talk once Rex is ready to transition."

The wheels were officially set in motion. Over the course of the next several months, there were brief conversations, delays, and hurdles to overcome, but even though things were moving more slowly than planned, it was all coming together for John to get his chance to really make a difference.

A few months before things became official, Reuben met with John. After the usual pleasantries and joking between the two men, Reuben took a moment and said, "John, something isn't quite right. I think I am having some issues with my heart."

John, knowing Reuben's affinity to bust chops and have his chops busted, had a quick retort, "I didn't think you had one."

Reuben's trademarked sly smile came across his lips. He chuckled with relief knowing that this conversation would be filled with genuine personality and not the uncomfortable pity and silence that others had previously shared. "Well I can tell you that I now have visual proof and I do have one. It's cold and black, but it's there," Reuben replied with his smile growing across his face.

"The problem is they can't figure out what is happening and I have more tests ahead."

John, with an open heart and a moment of seriousness said, "Reuben, you know that if you need anything, I mean anything, you just -"

Reuben quickly interrupted, "I know John and thank you, but now that we have that out of the way, I want to schedule a meeting for next month. It's time to begin to make some moves to finalize our discussions. I want to bring you in to meet with our leadership team. You know most of the team, but we have someone new, I'm sure you heard of him. His name is Andy Hoover. I've seen Andy in presentations and his philosophies are solid. You two will get along very well and he will be a great resource for you."

John was excited to get things finalized and to move forward. He was excited to meet Andy. "Reuben, just let me know when and I'll be there."

The two left with a handshake and a hug.

Reuben's integrity was second to none. Not only did he work to make sure that students were empowered and inspired, he always made sure to provide opportunities for his employees to grow. As in the case of Rex, he bent over backwards to make sure he kept his dignity intact while helping him land his dream job. Reuben's actions spoke volumes as to who he was and what he valued: people.

A month passed and it was time for the big meeting with the management team. Everything went very well and no one had any concerns with John. The team was excited to bring him in and see what he could do to improve the struggling school. They were ready to provide resources and support when necessary, but trusted him to lead. They were all on board, except Andy. Andy held some reservations and felt a bit threatened by John. He heard how the group trusted him and became insecure at having such a respected and viable leader under his supervision.

Andy struggled deeply with understanding people and had never been in a true leadership position. He knew this about himself and it ate at his self-confidence. Still, he knew that Reuben wanted John and he risked isolating himself if he opposed John's hiring. Now with all the proverbial ducks in a row, a few steps remained. The first step was to determine the timing of John's recommendation to the school board, approval, and announcement to the staff and community. This all would take several weeks with the contract details being worked out to everyone's satisfaction.

In the span of time before the announcement, there were a variety of phone calls and meetings between Reuben, John, and Andy. As Andy was John's direct supervisor, he was the go-between for the different departments to get on the same page. However, John received a call one day from Reuben. He knew it was a different call by the tone of the "Hey, John," when he answered. Reuben needed to meet with him as soon as possible. Something seemed amiss, but John hoped he was over analyzing things. He told himself that this was just a prep meeting before the final approval of his contract.

It was an overcast day as John pulled up to Reuben's house. Reuben's youngest girl came to the door and let him in. "Daddy! John's here."

John smiled at her proclamation and walked into the family room where Reuben had a gin and tonic at his side and a basketball game on TV. "What's up my friend?" John's voice boomed with hope as he shook hands with Reuben.

Reuben loved John's persona, so lively and filled with the warmth of friendship. "I'm wondering if these guys can ever make a shot that isn't a dunk," Reuben said.

John was never one for the game of basketball, but he shared his favorite story of how his job on his high school intramural team was to foul people and grab a rebound or two along the way.

During the course of John's animated storytelling, Reuben's face deteriorated into a sullen state until John read the non-verbal cue and fell silent. In decisive succession, Reuben stated, "John, tests are back. I have ALS. I have to resign at the next board meeting. You will be recommended and approved. Then the board will approve a motion to grant me disability leave."

John was stunned and saddened; he couldn't care less about the job at that moment. All he could think about was his friend, his little girls, and the grim inevitability of his condition.

Reuben continued, "We have to move fast and get this done."

John held back tears as he lowered his head and sunk into the couch. He wished he wasn't in this place and time. He was praying that this wasn't really happening. He internally begged to wake up, but this was no nightmare. "How long?" John quietly asked.

"It's not good. If I'm extremely lucky, five years, but they think it will be less than three," Reuben said with strength only the afflicted could muster.

Reuben was no victim; he was a man of great faith in God. He did not fear the inevitable publicly or privately. Reuben's only concern was for his wife and their wonderful girls. He wanted to make sure that the girls knew what they needed to know about faith, love, life, and family. Reuben would devote his final days to making sure of it.

After a few moments of Reuben consoling John's suppressed but obvious devastation, Reuben said, "John, I need you. I need you to turn that place around. There are good people there who deserve better. This isn't just work to many of them, it's their life and passion. They deserve better. No, they deserve the best and I know you will do everything you can to give them your best. There are people there who have lost their way and forgotten why they came to work here. Do what you can to help them rediscover this, but don't sacrifice the kids at their expense. What we provide our children is too important to them and their families. They will trust you. They will rely on you to do what is right. It will be extremely difficult, but it will be worth it."

John, still stunned and saddened, asked, "What would you expect the timeline to look like?"

"John, I would expect the ship to start turning around at six months and for there to be a complete turn around by the end of three years."

Although the job didn't matter to John in these moments, his loyalty to Reuben would be entrenched into his future focus. This was the last directive his dear friend would give to him: turn it around.

John and Reuben spent the rest of the time talking about no particular topic, just friends having a chat. Knowing that their time was limited to a few years, they did their best to ignore the inevitable. John left Reuben's home knowing the challenge that lay before him, but it was now wrapped in a last request type of heaviness.

The drive home seemed endless, as he was in a state of shock. John began to think. He vaguely remembered who he once was and why he began this journey. He remembered his desire to inspire, his focus being on things greater than numbers and test scores. He thought his previous self was naive and rolled his eyes at the foolish person he believed he once was. John began to develop a laser focus on this drive home. Improve the numbers, build a team, and weed out the negative.

John told himself this was the battle he was waiting for – to build his legacy. This was the opportunity to show everyone that he was a leader, that he was worth it, that he was more than just a funny guy. He became enveloped in the thought of being a great leader. John was determined to vanquish the ghosts of his past failures as a student, child, and young man.

He reflected on the extended path he took through his college years. John would make everyone, especially his parents, proud they invested in his lengthy journey to get a college degree. He would look down upon all those who privately but noticeably snickered at the length of time it took to graduate. He remembered those who believed he was a lazy drain on his parents. John whispered to himself, "This is the moment I have been training for. This is the moment I will rise to the occasion and reward those who believed in me and laugh at those who judged me."

CHAPTER TWO
FEAR AND STIFLING

For all of John's personality and fun, he had a serious and introverted side. Many people who exhibit these characteristics are considered ambiverts. Ambiverts are people who exhibit an equal blend of introversion and extroversion. Although many ambiverts are labeled extroverts by those who know them, the characteristics of extroversion can take a great toll on the energy level of the ambivert. As a part of being who he was, John had many sides to himself that were often confusing. He didn't quite know who he was supposed to be; the many different aspects of himself were consistently tugging at his heart and head for attention. He was creative and thoroughly enjoyed music, and although not blessed with the voice of an angel, he spent his time alone writing lyrics and recording melodies by voice. John hid this side of himself. He felt he needed to appease what he believed was expected of a leader and a "guy" growing up in a mid-sized blue collar town. John wanted to talk about nature, dreams, creativity, and spirituality, but he felt alone in those interests. He was a dreamer and a thinker, who heard the world and society telling him to be tough and put away those silly, non-profitable desires.

The messages came through the media, high school teachers, friends, coaches, and television. He heard adults discussing people who struggled to make money in their areas of interest. The conversations were focused on shaming and ridiculing the people who dared to live in their gifts; they saw their dreams as frivolous and unworthy. They wanted to see them fail, perhaps because living in their gifts seemed impossible to them or perhaps it would be an indictment on their lives of settling for money over purpose.

John was reticent in doing anything performance-related unless he was doing it for humor. Humor would meet the demand of what society had placed upon him and the myths he told himself regarding what he believed people expected of him. John struggled with how serious his heart felt, but he decided to seek the approval of his peers and the world around him. He would later regret not expressing what was in his heart.

John's parents were extremely supportive and encouraging towards his dreams, but even with them, he stifled himself. He had a secret side that he was extremely fearful of sharing. John knew his parents would be accepting and enthusiastically supportive. However, the world around him was teaching him to live in fear when it came to his interests and gifts. He knew his dreams would invite ridicule. These voices became louder than anything else he could have heard. If he went his own way, the amount of vulnerability and potential rejection was too much for John to bear. He buried everything he thought he could be.

John replaced himself with a person that society would accept.

A person who the world would respect. A path that would lead to his own disillusionment, disconnection, and distress.

John desired to be cool, he wanted to lead, and he thought he could help people by leading correctly. As he looked further into leadership, he joined the rest of the world in glorifying the position and the impossible standards that went with it. When John thought of leaders he thought of Generals, Presidents, Civil Rights Leaders, and more. Yet, he didn't see them individually and neither did society.

John and society meshed all the great leaders into one. One impossible standard to meet in order for your life to achieve greatness and to make a difference. He strongly wanted to make his life worthwhile; he wanted to be the next great person. The most interesting aspect of this was that John didn't initially want this for his own glory; he desired to do what was right for others and to help make the world a better place after he was gone. John wanted his life to matter for others.

Because of this and the sacred trials of the traditional high school experience, John was a wanderer in his final days of high school and during his years of college. He struggled greatly with the path that he was supposed to take in life. John didn't want to exist in a job; he craved purpose, a higher calling, a dare-to-be-great moment and profession for his life. John left high school being so diverse in interests, potential areas of strengths, and a range of possible personality and job matches, that there was no ideal fit for him. John's path was not so easily set and he felt lost.

After taking a multitude of guesses and after discussions with others regarding career pathways, he settled on the extremely purposeful major of "undecided." It was during this time that he explored. John took odd jobs for little pay; he delivered pizza, he worked in retail sales, and he volunteered to coach high school football.

The coaching position felt like it held a connection for John. He could invest in others and the sport that he loved growing up. An opening was available as a student assistant at the university John was attending and he was fortunate enough to get the position. The doors to being a college coach were opening and John dove in with full effort. It was through this experience of going to class all day, talking to career college coaches, and working countless additional hours at the football facility, that he realized the life this game held was not fulfilling for him. The prospects of moving every couple of years, spending 90-95% of his waking hours working on football, and missing the majority of his future family's life wasn't for him.

However, if the college ranks weren't the right fit, maybe coaching high school would work just fine. Yes, he knew that was the path. He would be a high school football coach. He would change the lives and trajectories of young men for the better. In doing so, John would also have to teach. This wasn't his heart's cry, but if it got him to coaching, then so be it. John decided he would be a coach who also happened to teach. That moment and this decision would set John on a path that would eventually lead to the opportunity presented by Reuben.

John entered his newfound potential program with some focus, but after several years of wandering through different options, he just didn't have the energy. He spent his time outside of college working, coaching, and finding Denise, the young lady who had captured his heart. His time in college became a war of attrition.

The only thing that motivated him was the thought of being able to marry Denise. Every moment writing papers, finishing projects, or studying for tests was done in the pursuit of his love for her and their future family. A strange occurrence happened during this process of pushing toward the finish line. John reversed his thinking about what he was going to be. He didn't change his major, but his focus.

Throughout the experiences he had in the classroom, John spent his time drawing up football plays and talking with athletes. He had an immediate connection to these young men. They were enamored with the fact that John spent time with a university program. In John's mind, he was just putting in his time to get his degree and his teaching certificate. After all, he was less concerned with the subject and more about coaching the game of football, because football was representative of life. Football had taught him powerful life lessons such as, overcoming adversity, learning from failure, and working to create greater opportunities. John initially believed this was a higher calling for him than the classroom.

However, as John began to see and feel the impact of what society and many times, education, did to him in limiting what he was to be in life, he started to see himself in students who weren't in sports. He observed and reflected on the struggle seen with students who don't fit the mold or have the dominating personality to play up to the teacher. He saw and felt a connection. John was looking for his chance to inspire children who were being forced into a role that they were never meant to play. His focus was no longer to be a coach who had to teach, but a teacher who was also a coach.

As John inched closer and closer to graduation, he felt the pull to open up the walls of the classroom. He understood the responsibility to not just teach a subject and make certain that students learned its content. It was his job to support and engage with each student. John had the power to fuel students to reach for their possible tomorrow, to elevate their trajectory, and ultimately watch them rise above what society and education consistently deemed was possible for each one. John wanted students to know that all aspects of creativity and individuality were appreciated and needed in this world. He wanted to awaken the phoenix in each sullen student who was imprisoned by traditional education and societal stereotypes.

Finally, with brute force and determination, John graduated college. He began his career with the intent and focus on inspiring students to use their gifts, find their purpose in this world, and do something great with it. He practiced what he preached as best as he could with the limited tools of anyone who was new to the profession. John made several mistakes along the way, but he also inspired the rise of many students. He was the thorn in the side of educators who wanted students to be responsive robots. He was a guide of hope for the cast-offs and disillusioned. He was a supporter of expanding appreciation and perspective for the students who flourished, but felt school was just a hurdle to be overcome. He taught and led with heart. John had a clue, for a minute.

CHAPTER THREE
DRIFTING ASLEEP

When people fall asleep, they often do so quietly, progressively, and sometimes have bouts of swooning themselves awake to fight the impending slumber. As John looked back on himself and the days that progressed towards his sleep, he thought of his father watching golf on Sunday. John's dad would often watch with staunch regularity and enthusiasm. He wasn't sure if the enthusiasm was more for the sport or for the nap that the sport brought on.

    John's father began very alert and intent on watching the entire match from his chair. With the remote in hand, his grip would slightly loosen, his head would begin to bobble back and forth until a continuous stream of snoring enveloped the room. In his younger days, John would attempt to take the remote and change the channel. This always resulted in a brief wake up and a muttering of, "I was watching that. Put that back on." Even if John could sneak the remote and change the channel, the snoring was so deafening that the volume of the TV could not compete. The room would eventually become deserted.

This was similar to John's experience. He began with hope, inspiration, and love, but gradually, he tired. Subtly, he began to fall asleep. The sleep fell upon him as he struggled with how students and teachers were being measured by test scores that had no capacity to define their potential or success. The distraction that these instruments had created in education was destructive. It limited the ability for everyone to understand the true potential of each student, and when coupled with governmental policies that devalued his purpose, John became increasingly frustrated.

With students who were living in near hopelessness and negative educators who were more concerned about a paycheck, their comfort, or a test score than the culture of their classroom, John's frustration grew. It pushed John into a self-righteous and combative state. He didn't know it, but with good intentions, he was slowly becoming something he didn't want to be.

He felt compelled to make a difference and change the system further. He wanted the power to call the shots and rid education of these albatrosses and infections. He believed that this was the legacy that would make his life worthwhile and provide a lift for those who would fall under his sphere of influence. He slowly drifted his eyes from inspiring and connecting, to gaining the power to defeat the enemy and win the fight.

John became hyper-focused on doing what it took to get his leadership credentials. He voraciously attacked his quest to get a master's degree in educational leadership. After being a meandering and terminally average student in high school and college, John began his quest to prove all those who doubted him wrong.

John set a blistering pace of courses. He took a program that is normally completed in six semesters and completed it in three. He often took two and three courses at a time, finishing each one with an A. When John finished his program, he had developed a reputation for being a hard charger who was willing to take on a challenge.

His goal was to be the best, but his ambition turned his eyes from his original purpose. If he could change education, students would have a greater chance at success. He didn't care what they chose to be in life, but he wanted each student to have a choice and not have a life put upon them. Although an incredibly noble reason for beginning this pursuit, it would have a cost associated with it.

John was blessed to get his first leadership position as an assistant principal at a large high school in Central Indiana: East View High School. It was on the east side of Indianapolis and had a tough but extremely loyal community. He belonged to a team of two other administrators who were led by the principal, Steven F. Green. Steven was a fun-loving, politically savvy, and intelligent leader who was making positive waves across the district with his ideas and student programs.

John and Steven quickly established a close mentor-mentee relationship. John was willing to take on any task even if he was already swimming with more than he could do. He would spend hours outside of the workday attacking problems that were brought his way. He was riding high and learning a great deal.

As John was beginning his climb up the leadership ladder, Denise gave birth to twin girls, Jules & Isabel. She understood what John was focused on doing and she approached it as a team endeavor. Her support meant the world to him. She gave John a heart and soul that he never had. Her love made him brave and tenacious. Unfortunately, this bravery didn't bring with it a strong focus on the needs of his home. John continued to rationalize the time spent away from his wife and children as a sacrifice to his legacy, the opportunity for a greater paycheck, and a chance to build his own self-worth. John was banking on the future while neglecting his family's present. He thought, "It is more important for me to be there in the teenage years. I have to sacrifice now."

John was becoming blinded by his ambition to become a great leader. He listened to Steven, watched other leaders, and continually reflected on the aspects of where he could improve. He still held close his belief that this was for the students, staff, and the community. John knew he had something special to give, but he continually framed and contorted the application of this "something special" to meet what the world had told him would make the most impact.

In this quest for leadership greatness, John began to put away pieces of himself. The songwriting became choked out as a waste of time and was replaced by practical leadership opportunities. His appreciation of the arts was revealed only to Denise. He became increasingly un-accepting of many people due to their intolerable focus on their personal lives and their selfish lack of commitment to doing better in their jobs. To John, the job was becoming everything.

John took on the negative educators who didn't focus on the needs of students. He saw the damage they caused to their students and the reputation of the larger group of honorable educators. He entered the conflict to fight against those who gave education a bad name – a task that didn't go unnoticed by their superintendent. A man named Reuben.

John learned how to handle many volatile and violent situations, and he learned how to work within the system. This took him further from his heart's desire to inspire, produce hope, and build a connection. He punished more than he praised, he ascended more than he connected. He was rising up the ranks like a rocket, but his true self was swooning to stay awake. John was under the strain of becoming a leader who was worth following. His expectations of himself were becoming unreachable.

John knew he lacked fulfillment and something wasn't right in his soul. The person he was once was foreign. "I'm becoming something better," he thought.

CHAPTER FOUR
THE ROCK

Leadership has become an exalted position, a cult of personality in our day and age. Society looks down upon the doers and followers or worse, ignores them all together. Who wants to be the offensive lineman when you could be the quarterback? Who wants to be the president's secretary when you could be president? Who wants to be the roadie when you could be the rock star? Over and over again, society has devalued the importance of the supporters and followers. However, it's the doers and followers who share the leader's vision that bring it to fruition. Society has deified the leader and devalued the follower, yet the leader and follower are in a symbiotic relationship. They depend on and need each other to function. They are part of a whole and only together can they make a difference.

Imagine a leader who has no followers. Nothing gets done and you simply have a voice in the wilderness that amounts to nothing. In reverse, imagine a follower with no leader. They are a rudderless ship that sails without a compass. They work without a vision and descend into a chaotic work state that lacks cohesion and direction. They tend to stay in their comfort zones and their growth is minimal. Followers and leaders need each other; neither is more important than the other. They are teammates with different roles. What is a painter without paints? What is a musician without an instrument?

John was obsessed with leadership and providing a vision for others to follow. He wanted to do something special that would be remembered. He wanted a legacy worth leaving. He wanted his life to matter. The first opportunity arose for John to make his mark when a mid-size school had an opening for a head principal – West Rock High School, home of the Eagles. It was in a blue-collar community with many ethnicities represented within the school walls, but people there made it work. The reputation for openness and the celebration of many cultures was an attractant for John, who believed strongly that people had more in common than the differences they observed. He wanted to learn from this community. The staff had an inherent closeness that was forged through trial and John was the right fit. He was now the leader of the West Rock Eagles.

Getting a leadership position came with many pitfalls: being too trusting, developing overconfidence, and looking at the world from only one perspective can have disastrous consequences. It was at West Rock that John would experience them all.

John left East View with great support and appreciation for his work. The district leadership looked on him fondly and as he left for his last day he received a phone call. "John, I'm going to bring you back someday." John knew this voice all too well.

"Reuben, you know I would like that. I've had a great experience here, but I've got to get focused on West Rock."

"That's not a no. I'll take it," Reuben responded with a laugh. "I know you are going to do a great job. You better stay in touch and I really would like to bring you back." As they wished each other well, John knew that Reuben was serious, but he didn't know that the wheels were already in motion.

West Rock was in a tough area of town, but the community had great respect for the school. The countless hours the staff spent working for their children was appreciated by its families. It was a place that made things possible for children. John was proud of this reputation and he vowed to honor and lead it forward. As John walked into the building, he met two people who would become tremendous advisors and friends, Katina and Barry. Katina was a math teacher who was working on getting her administrative license, while raising four kids as a single mom. Katina had been through some trying times as she fought to jettison an abusive husband and stand on her own. Her laugh was infectious and her strength was unquestioned. Katina's work ethic was unmatched and was only rivaled by her loyalty. Once Katina believed and trusted in someone, she believed all the way. She would fight tooth and nail for those she trusted and loved. Katina had John's admiration on her reputation alone, yet he could never foresee the impact she would have on his life.

Barry was the heart and soul of the school. He had an almost mysterious power to calm and connect with every student and parent who walked through the doors. His ability to understand the needs of people, and immerse himself in meeting those needs, established a reputation for being one of the most beloved members of the school community.

John met both of them a week after school ended for the summer. They needed to discuss needs of the school and he wanted the full tour. The meeting started with formality, but all three had the ability to dismantle formality quickly and the meeting became a chance to get to know new friends.

As Katina and Barry were giving John the tour, the three walked past the main entrance. John caught something out of the corner of his eye. He knew that flash; it was the lights of a police car. Katina and Barry continued walking as John slowly walked backwards to see if he imagined the sight. He then slowly walked forward again and saw the flash a second time.

"Hey! Take a look at this!" John barked.

Katina and Barry wheeled around quickly and walked back to where John stood. They peered out of the main entry window and there sat a group of young men on the curb. Several police cars had been called to the front of the school as a neighborhood argument became a group fight.

"All former students," Barry said with a heavy heart.

Katina quickly followed with, "Welcome to your new home." She then emphasized, "This is what we are fighting against. A neighborhood who has a great heart, but struggles with violence, drugs, and poverty. A population of students who strain to maintain hope and at times succumb to drugs or crime. They are preyed on by people who already live in despair. We fight every day to make certain they have hope." As sad as the situation was, it was a fitting beginning for John's tenure at The Rock.

Despite the unceremonious beginning, John was not fazed. He threw himself into the work of being the leader of West Rock. The long days that began at 7:15 AM and often ended after 9:00 PM continued to fuel his belief that he was sacrificing to do something special. His little ones and wife lived almost completely without him. In previous roles, when Sundays would begin to darken and the hour drew late, Denise would ask John what nights would he have to work late. Now with John in a new role, that conversation changed. Denise would now ask if she would see him during the week. She was increasingly living separate from John and although her loyalty didn't waver, her heart hurt. The distance grew. She was becoming angry at being the sacrifice for John's legacy. Denise would swallow her anger as best she could, but their connection was straining.

John wanted to tell Denise all that was happening, but that meant reliving his day and his day was less positive in this new role. John served as the complaint department, he struggled to lead those who had bitterness in their hearts, and he witnessed great kids with tremendous potential become swallowed up by hopelessness, depression, and anger. John was never more grateful for Barry and Katina. Their steadying influence and positive affirmation, along with the ability to find humor in any situation, allowed for needed stress relief. John began to realize that no matter how long someone watched the leader lead, no one could be prepared for the challenge, negativity, loneliness, and struggle that came with the job. It was never in the job description.

The negativity was most evident to John early in his tenure. In his beginning of the year staff meeting, after spending days with the building leadership team, John and the team formulated goals for the year. He was proud of the work that was done and was excited to share with the staff. If any questions were raised, people would do so in a real, but positive way. After all, the reputation of this staff was centered on being real and positive.

When John finished presenting the goals, he was bludgeoned with question after question that was neither positive nor constructive. John was unaware that the negative group would use his reputation for confronting underperforming staff members as a means to create fear amongst the staff in the summer months. This small but talkative group spent their time referring to John as a henchman brought in by the district to get rid of people. This could not have been further from the truth, but when dealing with negative people, the truth is never an obstacle.

Accusations began to fly at John about driving his own agenda. He was surprised and flustered. He was looking for help from the leadership team but no one stepped forward. After waiting, to no avail, for the members of the leadership team to step forward, Katina spoke.

"John, didn't you create this with the leadership team? Have others in this meeting seen this plan prior to today?"

This was the catalyst needed as John answered each question and then members of the leadership team meekly confirmed his answers. What John didn't know was that this ambush had little to do with him. Previous decisions made by the district left members of this negative group seething. In their minds, John was the closest they could get to hitting back at the district. Adding to the mix were the ongoing contract negotiations that were beginning to take on a harsher tone, contributing to the misdirected anger of the ambushers.

John was wounded and angry, and Katina was furious. John made the decision that he would not be hurt again. He thickened his skin and further hardened his heart.

As John moved forward to protect himself, his quest to eliminate vulnerability began to have a cost. His began to forget why he wanted to work in education in the first place. Darkness fell upon his original purpose.

Throughout the year, John gained wisdom and experience and he spent more time away from home, regularly logging in a minimum of five nights a week, working 12-14 hour days. John's family life was minimal and his girls did not miss him when he left for work. They were conditioned to his absence. Seeing Jules and Isabel becoming used to not seeing him seared his soul.

"Just sacrifice now so I can be there later," he would think to himself. John's friendships outside of his work life became more distant. His closest friends could not count on him being at get-togethers or events. He was drifting further from the shore, falling deeper into his sleep. He felt the strong thing to do, the manly thing, was to ignore the pain and get tougher with himself.

But at the same time, he was also gaining respect in his building. His decision-making, although inexperienced, was gaining trust. He built relationships with many parents, students, and staff members. He spent time listening to those who had ambushed him at that early meeting. John believed in order to lead, he needed to invest in the lives of his people. This investment had to be demonstrated by action. Still, he knew that the person he once wanted to be seemed less possible. He remembered his days working at the football office where he believed that his future family was more important than the possibility of being a football coach. He remembered believing that working more than 60 hours a week was incompatible with the family he wanted to have. Yet, here he was about to go to Saturday night basketball after spending the day working to complete evaluations and answering the hundreds of emails awaiting his response.

John was growing a seed of bitterness within his own heart. He believed people were stealing his energy, his soul, and his time. They cared not for the implications in his world. The constant neediness and self-centeredness made him wonder if the people to whom he was so committed to showing his appreciation and attention would care if he lost his family. Their constant demands led to a monopolization of his life.

"I knew what I signed up for. I will be 'The Job' and make a difference for everyone," he would tell himself. "They need me. I need to suck it up and quit feeling sorry for myself. This is leadership."

John left his office after working for four hours, the JV basketball game was set to begin. He made it right before tip off and spent time making sure everyone working the event felt appreciated. John would make time to have personal contact and laugh with each person working. During these moments, it was not uncommon for anyone with an agenda to pull John aside with a proverbial quick question. On this night he would get several of these, none of which had anything to do with the betterment of the student experience.

Basketball has a way of lasting forever during foul-ridden games; it seemed as though this night would never end. As 9:00 PM approached and John realized he had forgotten to call his family to say goodnight, he experienced a moment of sadness and regret. He knew this pace couldn't last. John thought if he was only left alone for a moment, he might be able to make this work on some level. He replayed all the conversations of the night and knew he should have broken them off to call home. John's inexperience was showing, even in his thoughts. His self-talk was rapidly growing more negative in regard to himself and others.

Finally, as the end of the varsity game was within sight, John stood against the wall of the gymnasium. His PTO president, Bill, flanked him as they were having a casual conversation about school and the experience of Bill's son.

As the game ended, Bill asked John, "Are you going to be around tomorrow for the lift-off sessions?"

"No, Bill, it's Sunday and I am going to be home."

"Really?!" Bill expressed some frustration in his voice.

"Yeah, one of the assistants lives nearby and he is going to come in and do some work while that's going on. Why do you ask?"

"I think you should be here," Bill responded.

"Bill, why would you think that? It's not even a school or school-related event."

"Well pardon me for saying this John, but I think that if there is an event at your building, you should be here. Just my opinion."

John was pretty well known for his diplomacy, but anger swelled inside of him. He felt the heat rise up his neck and towards the top of his head.

"Don't respond," he thought to himself. John thought of Denise, the girls, and forgetting to call. He thought of the 70-hour work weeks. He thought of all the inconsideration shown to him on a daily basis. John would not let this slide.

"Bill, where are we?" John asked.

With a laugh, Bill answered, "The basketball game."

"Bill, where is your son?"

"Right there on the court playing small forward," Bill replied.

In a moment of controlled anger, John gritted his teeth. "My kids are home right now wondering where their daddy is tonight and why he isn't there to tuck them in."

A silent and uncomfortable pause ensued until Bill spoke, "I'm sorry. I didn't think of it that way, John." Bill knew he over stepped his bounds.

John replied, "It's fine, but understand that I'm here being a good principal at their expense." As Bill looked towards the ground, John decided he'd had enough.

The timing couldn't have been more perfect as the final buzzer sounded and the crowd began to exit. John went to the center of the floor to make certain everyone left without incident. However, that conversation would stay with him.

As John drove home, he asked a question of God: "No matter how much I give, they will always want more. When I have nothing left to give, they will move on. What will be left?"

John hardened his heart further. He started to care more about his legacy; he needed to make this count. He was sacrificing too much of himself and his family. It can't all be for nothing. The seeds of bitterness and a "me versus the world" mentality developed. He knew he needed to find his legacy moment. Time and people weighed on him.

Denise continued her steadfast support of John's mission and drive towards his legacy. She remained dutiful and loving as she hid the anger growing inside. John was spending more time at work and with his bosses. He realized that to climb the ladder, relationships were important. He genuinely liked them and didn't pretend when it came to agreement or disagreement. He wasn't a "yes" man and this was greatly respected. Unfortunately, John was forsaking the relationships that mattered most in exchange for the world to see his greatness.

Denise loved her husband, but the distance between them was growing. She worked to connect and engage when John talked about his work, but alas, John wasn't a fountain of conversation. He often came home, plopped on the couch, and spent his final waking hour with the television as his focus. Denise would try and ask about John's day and she would try and share her own. She wanted to connect the dots between the two. John's eyes would roll, he would pause the television, and stare through Denise when she would talk. Eventually, she would give in and silence would fall upon them. Her heart hurt. John hated himself for his reaction, but his final drops of energy were often spent making the drive home. He had nothing to give to his family. Denise became angrier. She began to believe that the man she married was fading.

John's commitment to his legacy never wavered, but he was beginning to feel the demands of work and those around him were unquenchable. He wanted to be everything to everyone and strongly believed that the sacrifices would be worth it in the long run. John believed that his quest was good and that he was giving of himself, but he always felt as though he was coming up short. Then, in a moment of opportunity, Reuben called.

CHAPTER FIVE
THE LEGACY AWAITS

As John went through the process of meeting with Reuben and realizing that this was his opportunity, his moment to build a legacy, his excitement was palpable. First things first, he needed to set expectations and begin to develop relationships. He wasn't going to allow vulnerability and blind trust the chance to ambush him again. He would be a stronger leader, one with vision who would stand against those who would derail the mission to make Hyde Park Middle School a place that provided an opportunity to all students. John entered Hyde Park with a simple focus: to make sure that no matter what a student did or did not bring with them to school, the future was theirs to command.

John said to his students regularly, "If you leave Hyde Park, graduate high school, and you go flip burgers for a living that is fine by me. Any work is honorable and fulfilling no matter where it is. But if you do work in fast food, it is because you choose it. Not because it was the only option you had available. Education provides options for your life. Don't let life happen to you, make your own way."

John needed to have a solid team behind him. Dan was an

amazing guidance counselor and grew up in a blue collar town similar to John. They bonded immediately. Their conversations were honest, but Dan's kindness and appreciation for others always made him phrase issues in such a way that he could find the silver lining. John would come to not only appreciate this, but he would rely on Dan's mindfulness to see him through when times were stressful.

John immediately hired Katina to be his assistant principal. It was a dream come true for both of them, as they wanted to continue working together, and Katina's possibilities for promotion were logjammed by political garbage at West Rock. The fear of a strong, independent female scared many in leadership positions at their previous district, but John had a level of respect for anyone who was strong of mind. Katina was the perfect friend and teammate to bring to the team. Her experience and drive would carry them many times over in the next few years. She never truly realized her importance, but John knew her contributions were invaluable.

The last person to make up John's administrative team was an amazing confidant, who was also the building secretary. Rosa's job performance was only overshadowed by her high character. She would often prove herself as the backbone of the building, and this was not lost on John or Katina. Rosa's reputation preceded her and they would see her live up to that reputation time and time again.

John felt as though he had the makings of a phenomenal team. His opportunity to resurrect a school that was underperforming, reeked of a negative mindset, and had a "what's-best-for-me" philosophy was at hand. It was his moment to make a difference. John's time away from home would increase as he was now driving an hour in each direction. Denise grew more comfortable with being alone while John grew further away. They were heading down a path that led to greater isolation. John was losing his ability to feel pain; he was becoming numb. He was drifting deeper and deeper into his sleep. His heart was hard.

John tackled the foundational issues of the building, but he was beset with one problem after another. The teachers who had lost their way focused on and conspired to sabotage every move the leadership team attempted to make. They used every free moment in the day to coerce their colleagues and make things difficult, but what they didn't count on was the desire of many colleagues to see things improve. They were dedicated to their focus on the students. As staff became comfortable with John and Katina, they began to understand the high importance of integrity, loyalty, and honesty. They began to trust John and Katina because they didn't just say they would do what was best for their students, they walked their talk.

As trust was established, the communication opened between some staff and their new leaders. Reports of what the negative teachers were doing to be insubordinate and undermine the dearly needed progress started to flow with regularity. The staff members who were there to do right by their students and honor the trust given to them by the community began to speak up. They were honest with John and Katina, but they also began to take principled stands with their colleagues. They knew that if they were doing right by children, John and Katina would support them to the fullest. By their previous and current actions, the negative crew had lost influence. On the contrary, John and Katina were gaining credibility. The positive members of the staff were seeing how detrimental the negative crowd's efforts were to the building culture and, ultimately, towards the children they served. Their frustration became evident. A few representatives from this positive group approached John and Katina for a meeting.

In this meeting, they opened up to their leaders. They discussed their shared desire to engage in doing what was best for the entire building. They wanted to serve the community. They wanted to take a stand, and they wanted to stand behind John and Katina.

John sat and listened, containing his excitement over the fact that Reuben was right. Reuben said that there were good people here who just needed to be supported. They just needed to know they could stand up for what was right. After the group finished saying what they needed to express, Katina sat quietly. She had a knack for absorbing information and cutting right to the heart of it.

John started with appreciation and then shared his desire to see everyone, including the negative group, experience success. However, John couldn't help but see the negative group as the enemy. There was no middle ground with him. As he fell deeper into his sleep, he now lived in a world of absolutes. He was becoming bitter and combative, seeing people either as a friend or foe. He didn't seek to understand or provide true compassion toward someone he considered an enemy. His scope was limited by his mindset. This was not the person John wanted to be, but he was blinded by his ambition.

John walked a tenuous line of calling out his labeled villains, while he pledged his support for the group in front of him. Katina waited for her moment. When John paused, Katina cleared her throat.

"It seems as if these folks have become blinded by selfishness.

Their past experiences of bullying others in this building had given them power. That power is now gone and they are struggling with not being in control. They aren't evil people. I'm sure they still care about kids. However, we cannot in good conscience allow anyone to be bullied or to allow a culture of insubordination. We appreciate all you are doing for our kids and we will keep the lines of communication open. Thank you for being honest and open with us."

In one statement, Katina built a strong level of trust and credibility. Even though this group had come forward to solve problems and stand up to the negative group, they still saw them as people. John saw them as the enemy.

As the months went by, John and Katina were able to discern that the power of the negative group was held by three individuals. Bert (who was known as Skip), Priggie, and Mack. All three teachers were detrimental to the culture of the building and they often struggled with updating their professional knowledge. Now with John and Katina pushing for teachers to grow in their professional practice, they not only lost the power to make decisions for the building, but they realized that they were not the teachers they deluded themselves into believing they were.

Skip was the product of a bitter divorce that changed who he was internally. Once a positive leader in the building, he took his bitterness from the break-up of his marriage out on female staff members in aggressive and somewhat erratic fashion. He frightened many of the staff with his temper and with the manner in which he disagreed. John would not flinch at his antics, but Katina, after dealing with an abusive husband, set a tone with Skip when he tried to bully her. Needless to say, he never attempted to do it again.

Priggie initially had John and Katina fooled by her talk, but after hearing and seeing things that concerned them when they observed her classroom, they realized that she was in education for the attention. Her classroom focused solely on her interests. She used her platform as a teacher to discuss the events of her life on a regular basis. Priggie was less concerned about hearing students express their thoughts and feelings and more concerned about promoting how cool she thought she was to her students. Her influence in the building was predicated on the belief that she was a wonderful teacher as she talked an amazing game. Her practice was below average at best.

Mack was more difficult to handle. He openly spent time around John and Katina in an attempt to gain information. He would then use it to benefit himself and those he coerced into pushing against any new change. Mack was initially well-liked by John and Katina; he was used as a sounding board to get perspective and understanding. Mack was open about the shortcomings of the building. He talked about how he wanted change, but all the while, he was working to subvert the change that was happening. When John learned of Mack's true actions, he was furious at himself for allowing someone to fool him into trusting them.

Mack was the worst kind of foe in John's mind. He was negative and mean towards any new teacher who would say positive things about the direction of the school. With veterans, Mack was a master at using leading questions to attempt to draw people into negative thoughts and mindsets. He did not seem to desire to see anyone succeed. He wanted control of the decisions from the safety of hiding behind a facade and others.

What was worse than how Mack interacted with adults was the way he would isolate troubled or at-risk students. The students who had limited support and tended to not play school very well were targets for his disciplinary measures. They consistently felt his icy stare when they would ask for help. Mack was exceptionally polite and helpful if you were an A or B student, maybe even to a C student who could play the game of school compliance. However, if the student posed any significant need or challenge, Mack would write them off to be dealt with by administration.

John and Katina had no problem standing up for kids. They would strive to be tough and fair regarding any discipline that was needed, but they would also hold Mack to high standards of professionalism. This is where Mack couldn't hide from his true intentions and beliefs. John learned that people had a way of exposing who they were by their actions. They may be able to play a role for a time, but the true nature of people always finds its way to the surface. Mack was a good short-term actor, but a poor long-term one.

John and Katina were smart enough to play dumb in regards to the actions of these three. They wanted Skip, Priggie, and Mack to think that they were none the wiser. The game was fully on and John was determined to not just win, but to defeat them.

John was far away from who he wanted to be as a person, but he continued to rationalize his actions and position by looking for the end to justify the means. He felt he needed to engage in a strategic fight to make certain his life mattered. John needed to win to honor Reuben, to honor those who had supported and believed in him, to create a better experience for the children in his care, to establish a legacy of being the best in his profession.

John was in a deep sleep. He became bitter and he didn't know it. He was so completely grounded in being realistic that he missed the possibilities. He believed he had evolved into being a leader who thrived in his work. His work became his god. His religion was leadership. He slept.

CHAPTER SIX
THE GRIND

The work to build one's believed legacy is fraught with obstacles and battles. Steven Pressfield refers to these actions as "resistance" in his book, *The War of Art*. Pressfield discusses the process of creating something that serves the good of people. When you engage in this action, the forces of the universe balance this effort with struggle. John and his team were experiencing resistance. Early on in their tenure, most of the staff did not understand what they were doing. Icy receptions met their efforts to build relationships; people were standoffish and distant. John and Katina couldn't quite understand it. They were coming to people with honesty and integrity, but the doors weren't opening.

While they were struggling to make headway in the building, the district was drifting without leadership. Since Reuben's departure, the Board of Education was struggling to find someone to meet their expectations of leadership. As tough as it was to have no leader, John agreed with the process and respected the Board for looking for someone who was the right fit.

However, with no one in a long-term leadership capacity running the district, buildings and other district leaders began to go in their own directions. Andy, seeing the opportunity to force principals to engage in practices to promote his research and academic work to further his quest for personal recognition, took great advantage. He began to demand principals participate in practices that were counterproductive and veiled. A group of principals pushed against these practices for lacking transparency and authenticity. They knew they were just gilding the lily for Andy's benefit.

Andy's response was to instill fear in anyone who stood in his path to get what he needed. If someone openly disagreed with how he was doing things, they were subject to pressure and scare tactics. Andy hoped to gain power by using fear. This was not a tactic he could use effectively with men and women who knew that standing for their principles was more important than losing their self-respect. John stood firm.

Andy, already being uneasy with the strength of John's relationships, began to pressure him, and he was waiting for the opportunity to try and fire him. The problem was that Andy needed just cause or the district would be on the hook for paying John's contract for the next few years.

Andy attempted to bait John; he played good cop, bad cop, and worked to subvert some of John's efforts in the building. Unfortunately, anyone who supported John was a target as well. Katina was scraping by to maintain her home and provide for her children. Her deadbeat and abusive ex-husband was drinking himself into oblivion and wasting every dollar he earned. He owed back child support and Katina knew she would never see that money. She would juggle her bills each month as she determined which one she would take a late fee on and which one she would be able to pay. Katina had every justifiable reason to push John to comply with Andy's unscrupulous and clandestine efforts to advance himself at the expense of teachers, but she wouldn't. Her loyalty and friendship was rock solid. She was more concerned with doing what was right than she was about keeping her position. Katina stood by John and, by default, became a target as well.

As Katina and John buffered the building against the ethical battle going on at the district level, they continued to work to meet the needs of students and staff and attempt to build relationships within the building. John and Katina were developing great relationships with their new teachers and a few building leaders. These building leaders were not the ones with whom the negative group would originally trifle; they had emerged with the support of John and Katina from the drama that once shadowed the school.

However, the new teachers were a different story. They experienced regular, cold receptions and rooms that would fall silent upon their arrival. The undercurrent working against all the efforts being made to move the building exploited the newness of this group. When they made positive strides or attempted to make a difference for their students, they were treated like the monkeys moving up the ladder. John and Katina just couldn't find out where the cold water was coming from.

They understood why some were bitter and angry, but they never understood the attacking nature of the rumors. John looked back on his experience at "The Rock" and remembered the staff meeting ambush. He had to stand stronger than everyone. He needed to be a bigger target than the vulnerable new teachers. John and Katina were fighting battles on two fronts.

John had a third front to his battle. He started to realize what had been going on for a few years; Denise was living a life separate from his and his children were growing up with only a part time father. He was worried he was losing her. In his armored heart, John knew he couldn't blame her. One day, Denise called John at work.

"John are you sitting down? I need you to be sitting."

"Yep, I'm sitting. What's up?" he casually asked.

It was unusual for Denise to be so serious. John deluded himself into believing that he was doing this for kids and the security it would bring for his family, but the truth was that John was doing this for himself. It started with great intentions, but he became distracted and the motivation was changed. He didn't know where it turned, but he still knew he wanted to be great.

"Go ahead babe. I'm listening."

"John, I'm pregnant."

Silence gripped the air between Denise and John. She began to panic as there was no response. John stood against so many crushing pressures. He wanted to be a man of principles and ethics. John knew what to say, but the words were being choked from leaving his throat.

Instead he said, "Well, I don't know if I can be at the appointments like I was before. I mean, I work almost an hour away when traffic is good. I guess this is good news, right? I mean, I'm happy for us."

John immediately heard himself and thought, "I'm an idiot."

Denise responded with, "I hope you think it's good."

John could hear Denise suffocate her tears as she tried to stay calm about John's response.

"I'm sorry babe. I'm so sorry. I've just got so many things going on and I'm under so much stress. Can I have a do-over?"

Denise sat silently on the phone for a moment. Her sorrow screamed as she whispered, "OK."

"I love you, Denise. I'm so happy that we are having another child. You are such an amazing mom and wife. This child is so lucky to have you."

John knew he couldn't really have a do-over and his words would echo in his mind.

"Denise, I love you. I really do."

"I know and I love you too," John could hear the tears streaming down her face.

John knew they were there, but he convinced himself otherwise. The lack of visual confirmation allowed him to deny what he knew to be true. He kept telling himself that Denise wasn't hurt. She knew where he was coming from and that he was stressed out. Their call ended shortly thereafter, but it seemed as if it lasted hours.

When they hung up, John thought, "What the hell is wrong with me? Who have I become?"

He paused and thought, "What does it matter? We will turn this place around and I will be able to write my ticket to higher levels of leadership. I'll be able to get a job close to home and make great money. It will all be worth it."

John couldn't take a moment to think of the person he was.

If he did, he would be rocked to see how far he had drifted from his former self, the self that he really liked. He had degraded into a "win at all costs" leader who was willing to sacrifice family for the sake of legacy. John saw the work family as being critical, yet he couldn't see the importance of the family he had that lived an hour away. They needed him. Selfishly, John slept.

When John arrived home, he walked in with his usual demeanor of irritation and sapped energy. Denise had just put the girls to bed and she joined John to watch their favorite television show. She started to share about how the conversation they had earlier was difficult to move past. John, regretting his initial reaction, didn't want to relive his stupidity. His responses to Denise's perspective and feelings were a mix of simple acknowledgements of his actions. Denise was growing angry at the lack of depth and communication coming from John. Keeping a calm presence, she asked John to simply pause the TV and to talk to her. John sighed and pressed pause. His right to recharge was being infringed. John again engaged in stupidity.

"Look, I am sorry. That was a dumb statement. I already said I was sorry. Can't we just move on?"

Denise had enough. She took a stand.

"Move on! That's all you do. You move on from your family to your life at work. You ask us to stay in place, so you can conveniently be a part of this family when you want to and then when I have the audacity to open my mouth during your precious TV time to talk, you act like I am annoying you? John, you are becoming a complete narcissistic jackass. You keep telling me that this will be over soon and your legacy will be built and we can live then. But what about our lives in between? You want us to wait for you? Fine. I have committed to supporting you. I have been on the grind just as much as you. You know what I do at the end of my day at work? I don't get to go out and have drinks to climb the ladder. I don't get to go to staff functions. I don't get to go to events. I don't get to spend time with you. I am here creating a home for our family and I don't regret a single moment of that, but where is the person I married? If you think I am going to live with a person who disrespects me when I try and talk about how I feel, you better think again." Denise stopped short of telling John it was over. She was close to the end, but she knew the kids needed him.

"I will be loyal to you. I will support you. I will love you, but if you ever treat me like I'm some kind of doormat or annoyance again, I won't sit here and cry. I can guarantee you that. Stop being so damn selfish! Yes, you are tired, but so am I! At least for one moment recognize that I am working a whole lot harder at this than you are and give me some respect and effort! As far as having a do-over, unless you can roll back time and give yourself a pill to forget today, it's not going to happen. Those words you spoke to me will stay with you forever. You will have to live with it, not me! I'm not going to clear your conscience for you and absolve you of your selfishness and stupidity. Let's see if you can give yourself a do-over. Here's the big shocker John: I know you too well. You can't."

John's insides melted into a twisted, knotted ball of gut wrenching regret and anxiety. He knew every word from Denise was true. John wanted to defend himself, but he couldn't. His mouth was clamped by the truth. Denise has always been quietly strong; it was one of the things that drew John to her. She was no doormat. She understood sacrifice and John's vision for the future. She supported and believed in it, but her limit had been reached by John's disrespect. Her loyalty and love knew no bounds. John knew this. He had taken advantage for too long and Denise's patience had come to an end. John had to change, but he was being consumed by the monster of his legacy.

Denise dealt with the pregnancy with the help of friends and her family, as John continued to grind at Hyde Park. Approximately eight months after their conversation, Denise gave birth to John's son, Finn. Finn was a blessing.

John tried harder at home with little success. His lack of energy and self-centered behavior continued to creep in on a consistent basis. Denise and John would ebb and flow between times of anger, fighting, loneliness, struggle, and hints of hope. They missed the connection needed to experience joy. In their relationship, they moved from moment to moment, just trying to get by. Existence started to choke the life out of them.

CHAPTER SEVEN
SURROGATES

Over time, more staff members started to see that the focus that John and Katina were preaching and practicing was aligned to their own beliefs and, in many ways, aligned to their reasons for being teachers. They struggled to find why they didn't like them. The walls started to come down and real conversations started to happen.

However, one thing about John the staff couldn't understand was why he mercilessly teased anyone he liked. Growing up in a blue collar town, this was a sign of affection and genuine trust. They called it busting chops or giving each other a hard time. John never liked it growing up, but he became conditioned to it and spent years developing a quick wit and sarcastic tone to match that of his friends. As John desensitized himself and shut out feelings that would cause him to be vulnerable, he saw the value of sarcasm as he experienced the skin-thickening trials of leadership. John believed that he could love and appreciate people without being vulnerable and having to look weak by using words that seemed unmanly. John could keep the armor on while he was messaging his genuine appreciation for others. He was quick and harsh with his busting of chops. What he didn't realize is that others weren't speaking this language and their experience with him would be colored by this way of expression.

As he continued his grind to make Hyde Park a life changing experience for students and create a legacy worth remembering, and worth the price he was paying personally, real connections began to develop between John and several staff members. New hires and veterans alike began to be a part of John's surrogate family. John considered these people to be brothers and sisters in the quest to do something special, and cared deeply for each of them. A bond in the struggle was being created that went far deeper than the surface. As his family lived without him, John was increasingly lonely. He grew to see his role as the person responsible to not only push staff on their professional growth, but to also care and support them in their journey. John showed tremendous dedication as he began to lead with heart.

The struggle for the authentic John was coming soon, although he didn't realize it. He plodded forward trying to make his life worth living. He searched for success with test scores and innovative ways of doing his job. At the end of the day as John began to lead with strength, love, and caring, he needed his surrogate family to be more than just staff. After all, he was sacrificing the love of his life and their children for his work.

John's life became deeply invested in his staff, but at the end of the day, they went home. John would then spend his time in his office working alone. He continued to sleep deeply as the tide was turning. The building was showing growth and student achievement increased. John became obsessed with these scores and began to drive harder towards the goal of higher numbers. He found himself restricting enrichment opportunities for students based on their need for remediation in the so-called important subjects. John no longer looked to inspire and connect with students, he wanted to see them achieve. He wanted the scores. John wanted victory. It became a bottom line business.

As John's loneliness and thoughts of being victorious in his quest grew, Dr. Kirk Browning was hired by the Board of Education to serve as the district's new superintendent. Kirk, as he preferred to be called, was an old friend of Reuben's from college. Just like Reuben, Kirk would provide John with tremendous perspective and friendship. John had been without someone to challenge him in thought for several years since Andy was more concerned with his own gain and having people follow him without question. Besides, John had already crossed the line with Andy. John was concerned with growing teachers, while Andy was concerned with forwarding his own career. John wanted transparency in how he would operate, Andy didn't care for anyone's perspective, but his own. With Kirk leading the organization, Andy's reign ended.

John was fortunate that Kirk was a person with great integrity and honor, and had a heart for people. He took his time to gain an understanding of the people that served the district, to understand its traditions, operations, and the focus. He began to ask questions about why certain practices were in place. He wanted to be transparent in his practice with the entire community. It was this leadership that inspired John.

Kirk was easy to like. He was of average height and a bit on the heavy side, but his laugh and wit lightened even the most difficult of moments. Kirk had a way of getting to the heart of the matter and was able to see people for who they really were and understand their motivations.

Kirk was a man of great depth and gratitude. However, many saw him as a person to try and butter up in order to further their own agendas. Yet, he handled these folks with grace, firmness, and patience. Reuben had told John stories regarding the character of Kirk, but John was amazed by the volume with which Kirk's actions spoke. John couldn't help but to listen to the message of Kirk's life.

John's heart was hard, but something was changing. A feeling of being unsettled began to take hold. Kirk's influence and coaching caused John to reflect.

CHAPTER EIGHT
ELEVATION AND DESPAIR

The tide had turned. John and Katina were dealing with more desperate and overt attempts by Priggie, Mack, and Skip to stop the progress being made in the building. These attempts became so ridiculous and hateful that it was almost impossible to believe. One example was when Priggie spent time during an athletic event undermining the professionalism and intelligence of a new teacher. She was doing this to parents who had children in the new teacher's class. The parents were sickened by this open lack of professionalism and disrespect towards someone who had already developed strong relationships with their children, and several called John to report the incident. This eventually led to Priggie receiving disciplinary action.

Actions like these seemed to eat a great deal of time that John didn't have to spend on such matters, but he would not ignore it. He hit these instances head on and did what was necessary. Priggie finally had enough and resigned.

John was winning, but becoming increasingly aware of his weariness. He pressed on. He knew they were making progress and he couldn't allow the momentum to shift. Everything seemed to be moving in the right direction, then John received a call from Kirk.

"John, we have to get down there now. Can you leave?"

"Yeah, give me ten minutes and I'll be ready."

Kirk arrived at the school and John got in the car. They drove in silence to the First Lakes Care Facility. They walked in at a quick pace, but with gentle purpose, and saw their friend. Reuben struggled to talk. His mind was imprisoned in a body that would barely respond. Reuben whispered with great strain the following words, "You know what is important. I love you."

Kirk patted Reuben on his arm, "I know. You don't have to worry about us. We love you too."

John jumped in. He had to say it from his lips as well. "I love you too. No matter what happens, we will see each other again." The friends sat in a heavy silence with little to say. Their souls took comfort in being together. This would be the last time on this earth they would get to sit together.

The next Friday, Kirk entered John's office. He closed the door. "He's gone." Silence and tears flooded the room.

The next twenty-four hours seemed hazy to John. He could barely remember what took place before and after Kirk's visit. He was in pain and needed to find a way to control his world. He went to the office. As he sat down at his desk, John tried to get his bearings.

"Just do something," he thought. He opened his email and saw something from an unfamiliar address. Normally, he wouldn't open an email that he didn't recognize, but he was compelled to look at this one.

"The address seems normal enough," he thought to himself.

The email read, "Our greatest glory is not in never falling, but in rising every time we fall." John knew who it was from, but the skeptic in him prevented full belief.

He replied to the email and wrote, "Who is this?"

The email that was returned stated, "The email address does not exist".

He knew it had to be from Reuben. John felt this was the only possible option. He loved the quote and thought it had to do with his work at Hyde Park. But, Reuben was sending a message that would take John years to fully understand.

John's energy was crushed with the loss of Reuben. Although they had not been working together, John spent more time with him than he had in the past. Since Reuben had been stuck at home and at the First Lakes Care Facility, John made it a point to visit monthly. During his last six months, John and Kirk spent a great deal of time with Reuben. It was good to just be together.

Reuben's condition frustrated him when it came to conversation, but his mind was incredibly sharp. John looked forward to the opportunities to be together. It was a chance to learn from the two leaders he admired most and an opportunity to engage in some hilarious back and forth. That was all gone now. John struggled to understand why good things happen to bad people and why bad things happen to good people. He knew life wasn't fair, but the loss of his friend tapped into an emotion he had not experienced in years: genuine sorrow. John was becoming an angry, sad, bitter, and judgmental person.

Reuben's funeral was uneventful as the parade of colleagues who came to pay their respects sat emotionless. John wondered how could they sit there and not feel anything.

"We lost a good man. One of the best I have known," John said to himself, "and they seem to be unaffected."

John was never at the funeral of a public figure before. He didn't realize so many people who didn't really know his friend would show up because of obligation. They sat stoically. John's judgmental perspective rained down upon them. He became irritated by those who held their emotions. He gave no thought to how people mourn in their own way and how ultimately, they were there to honor Reuben. John gave no grace, no margin, and no kindness to those who didn't pay Reuben proper due in his mind.

As Jeff Buckley's version of "Hallelujah" was played, John eyes filled with water. As he sat amongst the stoic titans of his industry—superintendents, executive directors, and board members—John's sorrow was too much to bear. He wept. John felt Reuben deserved his tears. It was a fitting tribute to a man who had meant so much to him. The titans and their opinions were meaningless to John. Reuben was the only person that mattered.

John could not shake the image of the lack of emotion from the titans. Kirk's grief was obvious and real, but as the assembled left the church, he could hear and see that it was business as usual for the lot of them. He was angered at the perceived lack of appreciation for the person Reuben was and what he had done in his career. John screamed within his mind, "Can't we all take just one flipping moment to give a crap?!"

His emotions and thoughts were in a tortured tug of war. John was lost. The only thing that made sense to him was work, so John decided that he would honor Reuben. Hyde Park would be a tribute to his friend.

John became more intense than ever, often envisioning the day when all was accomplished. He dreamed of the joy he would feel. He pictured himself taking a copy of the school's testing results to Reuben's grave and leaving it as a tribute to his leadership and belief in John. As John continued to think on this, the image of people leaving the church going about business as usual haunted him. He thought for a moment about his own end.

John attempted to think about what was coming up for the following day but his mind would not allow it. The sights of the funeral stayed center stage. John started talking out loud in the car to drown out his thoughts. His refusal to open his spiritual and mental eyes for a moment was reminiscent of a teenager who was sleeping the day away.

It is late in the day and all efforts to get the teen to wake up have been exhausted. The parent, with no other recourse, goes to the window, opens the blinds, and begins to rock the teen's torso to get them to open their eyes to the light. The teen, desperate to stay in a state of slumber, may mentally wake up, but will tighten their eyelids and roll away from the light. Their refusal is stalwart and unwavering. The parent gives in and walks out. The teen, in their disdain for the light, gets up only to shut the blinds and return to slumber. This was John's battle as he drove home.

John tried to call a friend for distraction. No answer. It was John and reality in a showdown. Reality was opening the blind. It was shaking him; it was urging him to wake up. John was obstinate in his refusal. His eyes tightened, but reality was unrelenting. John turned up the music. He needed noise. He couldn't afford to give in and think about what reality was trying to show him. He arrived home exhausted and battered. John won this round, but the fight wasn't over.

CHAPTER NINE
SUCCESS, DISCONTENT, EMPTINESS, AND LEGACY

John needed a victory. He was tired of being lonely. He was weary of fair-weather friends within the profession that used their relationships to gain information and further their careers. Living in a world of false people and motives, he was so far away from who he was in his soul.

John began to feel it on a larger scale; something wasn't right. The legacy started to mean less as it was beginning to cost him more of himself. The challenge to build a legacy used to propel John forward, now it was devouring him. He would push himself to get stronger and tougher, but his weariness was evident. He relentlessly held on to his quest for a legacy and the chance to honor Reuben with his work, but his spirit grew more unsettled.

At the end of a particularly average day, John and Katina were talking about life.

John said, "You know, I wonder if there is more than this."

"Where did that come from?" Katina inquired.

"I don't know, it just…I just…I know that once we do this, we can find a better life. You will become the principal of your own building. Hopefully, I can get to a place where I can find some type of life. Well, maybe a life that isn't in this position. Hell, I don't know."

Katina sat quietly and unfazed. "You are doing great work here John and yes, when we're done here, we will find something that represents the next challenge. We're just tired."

"You're probably right Katina, but..."

"John, you know, I never took this job to become a principal. I took this job because I believe in you and I want to make a difference for kids. I know who you are, John. You can't let the job get to you. I'm not here for advancement, I'm here to support the person I see inside of you. You are bigger than this job. I know this."

John trusted Katina's perspective, but he started to become restless in his purpose and her words cut deeply to his soul. He was startled at the confidence with which she told him he was bigger than this job. He started to think about all the time and effort that he put into it. John wanted to find a way to escape the work. He needed a long break, but with three kids who needed food, clothing, and shelter, John was tethered to having a job.

John began to think on riches. How could he get rich? What could he do with the little time he had in the day to start a business that wouldn't require constant oversight? He started to read all the books he could find on getting wealthy. He began to believe the lie that money would find him happiness. John was beyond miserable, but he wouldn't let go of his mission. The job had to get done. The legacy was nearing completion. He had to finish.

John and Katina would experience outside resistance, but internally the team was finally humming at a breakneck pace. The staff felt John's love for them and they would do anything to make certain they didn't let him down. That meant going further for their kids than ever before. They gave it everything they had to achieve the dream of being difference-makers for all students. Katina's words would continue to echo in the caverns of John's soul. John's struggle was real.

As the school began to experience unified momentum, John had less conflict to deal with, and although he was still doing a great deal of work, his world was becoming quieter. As the volume dropped, the distractions lessened. John's mind began to fight with all the observations of the past few years. This time he could not silence its voice.

Finally, the school blew through its ceiling. The results were in. The students and teachers performed at the highest levels possible and led the district in almost every category of achievement and student growth. In a few long years, John and his team broke open the possibilities and captured the accolades that elude many for their entire careers. They were given awards by national education agencies, the state, and their board of education. John received recognition from parent groups and peers. But what evaded him was fulfillment. The bottom line of the business was victory, but John felt hollow.

John remembered the night that the testing results came in, when a friend of his called with the good news. John absorbed the news with relief. He felt as though he honored Reuben. He felt relief. He felt relief? Relief should not have been the feeling! Where was the joy, the excitement, the fulfillment? Where was his heart? What happened? Where was his spirit?

Reaching the top of this mountain, gaining this achievement

was supposed to be thrilling, but it was nothing. John began to process his emptiness. The world and society promised him long ago that if he changed to be the person he had become, this victory-driven workaholic who put the job before all else, that in the end, it would grant him fulfillment and joy. It would provide him a better life. It would allow him to find exuberance. The world and society lied.

John knew he couldn't approach his team without enthusiasm, so he had to hide his distraught soul. He needed to lead them in the celebration of what they had accomplished. John was very proud of what they had done for kids and the team they had become. Regardless of his emptiness, he needed to put on a false front and a face of excitement.

John shared the news with his team. He methodically informed those closest to him and then the entire staff. His excitement was contrived for he knew the victory cost him real connections in his life. He knew it cost him his spark, his enthusiasm, and nearly every ounce of the positive dreamer he once was, but at least his legacy was established. In the beginning, he thought that his legacy would make it all worth it.

"My life matters now," John thought to himself.

"But what's left?"

With the turn-around of the school complete, John had to face his mind. He remembered the funeral, Kirk's mentorship, the politics of the world he was in, the children he was helping, the ones he was missing at home, and the love of his life. John was living so far away from the woman he slept next to each night. He loved her deeply, but they were living at such a distance it was as if they were in different

SUCCESS, DISCONTENT, EMPTINESS, AND LEGACY

parts of the world.

John's unsettled soul started to manifest its displeasure physically. He was experiencing consistent headaches and they were causing some vision issues. During the school's routine wellness check, he was surprised to find his blood pressure was through the roof.

The nurse looked at him with big eyes, "Do you know you have high blood pressure?" John was stunned and answered that he wasn't aware of anything.

"Sir, your numbers are 190/120. I'm going to call the squad."

"Don't do that, I just got off the phone with a very angry parent and I was rushing to get here. I'm sure those numbers will go down in a few minutes. It's just a moment of stress." John pleaded with the nurse. She relented in her resolve to call the squad, but John wasn't being completely honest with her. Plenty of time had passed since the phone call and he was only semi-rushing to get to the wellness check. He was scared, but he wasn't a fool. He followed up quickly with his doctor, where he learned he had high blood pressure. John received a prescription and a caution to regain his health.

This incident made John think about his own mortality for the first time in his life. He spent many years thinking he could never fall at an early age; now, he viewed himself growing old too quickly. John took pause and he reflected, acquiescing to the voice of his soul. He began to allow it to talk and reality soon followed. This reality made John come to terms with the fact that he did not like the person he saw in the mirror. He didn't know himself. All of the accomplishments, heroics, and admiration didn't seem to make a difference. That man who stared back at John was foreign.

As John was building his legacy, the work and leadership of Katina was noticed across the region. Her ability to connect with people, her integrity, and especially her courageous focus to do what was right became admired. She was being recruited by several different schools from inside and outside the district to become their principal. After many interviews and offers, Katina was unsettled. She reached out to John for one last bit of advice. "What would you do?"

"What would I do?" he echoed back. "It's not what would I do, it's what feels right to you. You can't go by the numbers or by the reputation of the school. You have to go where it feels right to you."

"John. No, I mean, should I do this? Would I be a good principal?"

John replied simply, "No, you will be a great principal. There is nothing good about you. You are great. If you want this, take it. You have my full support no matter what."

Katina teared up and smiled. "Thank you," she said quietly. "I've loved working with you and you know we will always have each other's backs."

John replied, "Always."

Katina took a job that was in her home district. There, she would work to improve the educational experience of the children in her community and of her own children as well. It was more than she dreamed would happen, but what she would accomplish in her time there would transform the lives of many children, staff members, and families. Katina was in her purpose.

With Katina's exit, John decided that he needed a new challenge and to get closer to home. He missed his family and wanted to spend

SUCCESS, DISCONTENT, EMPTINESS, AND LEGACY

more time at home. With the legacy now built, John could afford to spend more time with them. His relationship with Denise was withering, and he needed to spend time tending to it. John didn't know if it could be saved, but he had to hope. He explained his perspective to Kirk and, with his blessing, John applied for another principal position. Though this school would leave him less than fifteen minutes from home, he was sad as he knew an era was ending and he would have to leave many wonderful friends who worked alongside him in the building. Through their care and love for children, John saw the light of how powerful a teacher could be for their students.

John would be forever indebted to his team and the people of Hyde Park. He believed his legacy was safe in their hands. The culture was established and students would reap the benefits for years to come. With relief, John was offered the job closer to home and took it. Unfortunately, a legacy and culture in a school are dependent on the leader and on their behavior. The leader that followed John revealed a truth that would prove to be a hard-hitting lesson: legacies are forgotten and cultures can be dismantled by a leader who lacks commitment, exploits fear, and chooses the path of personal comfort.

The leader that followed John at Hyde Park dismantled all that he, Katina, and the staff had accomplished. In less than a year, the staff was miserable. Their new principal didn't know their names, he took measures to humiliate and blame staff when he didn't follow through with district initiatives, and he pitted staff members against each other, creating a culture of fear. To add even more tension, he treated the women staff members much differently than the men. He used intimidation tactics when a female took a stand against his behavior. Eventually, this would lead to some fabricated story of how she was being insubordinate and would result in disciplinary measures being taken.

The new leader removed the high but reasonable expectations regarding student behavior and ownership. He wanted no parent complaints, no kid complaints, and heaven help you if you worked there and complained. In one year, nothing was left of the work that had been done previously. John was devastated. He wondered what it was all for and why God allowed this to happen. He wondered why he had wasted the past several years of his life. All the awards, accolades, respect, and measures of success were gone. He went from the top of the mountain and a strong sense of self-worth, to wondering how all of his hard work—his legacy—could be destroyed in such a short time. Even though John was in a different place, he hurt for the amazing educators and students being tossed aside. John's heart broke. He struggled to make sense of it all.

John struggled to deal with the realization that the past few years were now irrelevant. His legacy was a firework—splendid and awe inspiring for just a moment as it faded into the black sky. The only things that remained were a marriage on the rocks, children who didn't know their father, and a haunting hollowness within himself.

John decided to lead his new building differently. He still worked hard, but he understood that there were boundaries and work should not be life, drawing a natural conclusion after seeing all he worked for destroyed in a matter of months. He began to look for a life that he would enjoy. John struggled to tear himself away from work as if he was programmed to stay later than everyone else, but the pull of his children and the speed with which their life was moving was too much to keep him in his office. John began to fight for Denise and their life together. It was an uphill climb. Slow, but progressing. He continued to balance his habits and his desire to be present for Denise and their children.

CHAPTER TEN
A QUICK RUN

Working in his new school, John would find less pressure as he began to focus more on people than a legacy. On a day that began like any other, John would begin to see there was more he had to adjust. He started with his walk around the building saying hello to every staff member he could find. He had been battling an illness that was more than a cold, but less than pneumonia. This illness had been knocking staff members and students out for the last week. Even though John felt miserable, he believed it was more than critical that he went to work to lead the short-staffed building. When he came back from his walk and sat in his chair, something was amiss. His head felt strange; he felt unusually lethargic and powerless. John was a stubborn man when it came to the doctor, but he began to feel fear and the possibility that he was dealing with something he couldn't shake. He decided to drive to the urgent care down the road.

As he was about to leave, John yelled over to Brooks, his assistant principal, "Hey! I'm going to make a quick run to the clinic, be back in an hour."

"Want me to drive you?" Brooks shouted back.

"Nah, I'm good, but thanks." John walked to his car and started the engine. He was looking for his sunglasses as the sun was low in the sky and the light was blinding. He couldn't find the glasses, but realized it would only be a problem on the way back as the sun would be on his passenger's side and behind him during the trip.

John backed out of his parking spot and proceeded to the four-way stop at the exit of the school driveway. Traffic was nonexistent, but he waited a moment at the stop. As he was about to pull forward, he felt he needed music as he made the short drive. John called on his favorite playlist to accompany him. He looked up from his phone and made certain there were no cars waiting at the four way stop. As he checked each direction, all was clear and he pulled forward onto the street. In an instant, all went black as the world seemed to explode around him.

"Are you OK John?!" No response. "Call 911!" Brooks yelled to the secretary.

John was regaining some level of alertness, but was racked with pain. He didn't know what was happening. In what seemed like an eternity, John was comforted by a host of caring educators. He could only muster one meek word: "What?" He was embarrassed by whatever happened.

"John. You were in a crash. Don't worry, we're calling Denise." John knew the voice belonged to Brooks, but he couldn't think, let alone say another word. When the ambulance arrived, he was strapped to a gurney, placed inside, and whisked to the nearest hospital.

On the trip to the hospital, John thought of Reuben's funeral.

He wondered if everyone would go about their day after his own funeral concluded; would anyone weep for him? Would it matter that he was ever alive? He wondered what his kids would remember about him. He thought of Denise and how he loved her, but was absent from her life over the last several years. He wondered if she would be able to move on if he died today. John wanted to spend the rest of his life loving her the way she deserved to be loved, but was thinking now he may not get that chance. He missed his wife. In that moment, he only wanted to be with her and their children. John then began to believe that his life only mattered for the moment that he led Hyde Park to its accomplishments. He thought he was going to die and began to shed tears of regret. Then, he lost consciousness.

That night was a blur as John was roused from sleep every hour to be poked and prodded with needles. He remembered an article that discussed how important sleep was in the recovery process after any physical illness or trauma. Apparently this hospital did not believe in that premise. John was so tired. He acquiesced to each of the night nurse's demands for an arm every time they came in. The following morning, an exhausted John was visited by the doctor.

"Well, John how are we today?"

John was groggy, but not absent of his wit. "Well doc, since you're walking around and I'm lying here, I would say that average is OK. However, I feel like I was run over by a bus."

The doctor laughed and said, "It could have been worse, John. You could be gone. In fact, I don't know how you're doing as well as you are. This should be much worse. I honestly don't know how you made it."

John listened to the doctor as he told him about the crash and the injuries he had. "John, I have no idea why you are still here. Someone up there likes you." John, paralyzed by the news that he should not be alive, sat in silence.

The doctor continued, "Believe it or not, you'll be out of here in a couple of days."

"Doc, what about the other person? Was it my fault? I can't remember much. I just remember leaving to go to urgent care."

The doctor took a breath and exhaled. "Don't worry about that now. There will be time for questions, but for now get some rest and we'll talk later. Heal up so we can get you home soon."

As the doctor left, John lay there thinking about what his life was worth. He thought of his broken legacy and how temporary it was to this world. He believed that there had to be something more to his life. He started to think about what mattered most to him and the door opened. It was Denise with the kids. They all walked in rather quietly, thinking John may have been sleeping.

When they saw he was awake, the kids with cried, "Daddy!" and climbed on the bed to hug him. John's pain went from intense to excruciating as his kids squeezed him. He wanted to cry out and tell them to stop, but he bit his lip desperately, knowing that he almost didn't get to have this moment. A few seconds is all John could bear before he had to break off the hugs.

He eked out, "Lots of pain."

Denise got the kids off the bed and looked him in the eyes. They both wept as they stared into each other's soul. John wanted to say so many things to her. He wanted to tell her that he realized he almost lost everything that mattered for a seemingly temporary legacy. He wanted to tell her that it wasn't worth all the time lost and the distance between them. John wanted to apologize for not being the man she married. He wanted to tell her all this and more. The two cried while staring into each other's eyes; it was if she knew everything going on in his head. The thought of losing him was too much to bear. They may have been in separate worlds, but they were here now. Together. Her heart began to heal. His heart became hopeful.

As the nurse entered the room, she took a moment to watch the happy disaster that was unfolding. The kids were bouncing on the empty bed next to John and Denise. They watched them with teary-eyes. With each jump, Finn pressed the channel button on the remote. It was a mess of absolute joy. After taking all of this in, the nurse said for the kids to come with her to grab a snack at the nurses' station, sensing that Denise and John needed a moment. When they left, Denise kissed John's head with a gentle intensity that told John how happy she was to see him in a much better state than the previous day. John still couldn't remember anyone or anything. It was all a blur.

"Babe, do you know what happened?" John asked. "I only remember getting my keys to go to urgent care. What did I do? Is the other person OK?"

Denise began to cry. "It wasn't your fault, but the other driver didn't survive. The police told me last night. He was on his phone, speeding, and he ran the stop sign. You couldn't have seen him coming around the corner."

John's heart sank. No matter who was at fault, he realized that someone died. The guilt that it wasn't him began to permeate his thoughts. "How old?"

Denise knew the answer, but didn't want to share it.

"What matters now is that you are still with us."

"Babe, how old?" John was persistent in his questioning.

"Twenty-one." John began to sob. "It wasn't your fault. I'm just thankful that you are alive. It was an accident." Denise worked to console John, but regardless of the reasons why the accident happened, John was riddled with guilt.

"Why am I still here? Why isn't that young man alive? What the hell am I doing?"

Denise realizing John wasn't in his right mind, snapped at him. "You are here because I need you. Those kids need you. This world needs you. Wake up and see this as a second chance, a chance to make a real difference."

"That's all I've been trying to do. How the hell don't you see that?" John fired back.

Denise regained composure and, with deep love and kindness, said something that pierced John's heart. "You haven't made a difference for us yet. You haven't done what you were meant to do."

Frozen in discovery, John knew this wasn't just Denise talking to motivate him or snap him out of the guilt; this was a message from her heart. He let his head fall to the pillow as he exhaled. The kids returned to the room and brought their cheerful chaos with them.

The rest of the day continued with blood tests, general checking on John's well-being, and his kids begging to find vending machines. The family found enjoyment in the peace of being together. John completely forgot about the responsibilities of being a principal and focused solely on his family and their time together. For the first time in years, he was in the moment and this moment was powerful and healing. He needed to get some rest as the day was quite active, especially with the kids and Denise limited to the confines of his room. As dinner concluded and John received medication that would make him drowsy, the family said their goodbyes for the day. Denise leaned into John to kiss him good night. John reached his hand behind her head and kissed her gently at first, but with increasing passion. He kissed her more deeply than he had in a long time.

"Our kids are my world, and you are my heart." Denise smiled and walked backwards toward the door. Their eyes were locked on each other as they did when they first dated.

"I love you," was sent from her lips.

"I love you too, babe." The door closed behind Denise as the night was looming, and John drifted into sleep. Life was about to get real and the moon rose.

CHAPTER ELEVEN
RECALIBRATE

As John opened his weary eyes and the room came into focus, he saw that the wall clock told him that it was 11:11pm. He was stunned that the staff had let him sleep from 7:30pm until then without being disturbed. He checked his phone for messages as the screen blared light through the darkness of the room. John quickly shut his eyes at the obtrusive blast of light; he would have to do this gradually. Slowly, John reopened his eyes, waiting for their adjustment to the light. He checked a variety of apps and read through a few messages of goodwill and care. He knew he couldn't respond at this hour, but he hoped he would remember to do so in the morning.

John was now very awake. He struggled to think of what to do. He didn't want to watch television or listen to music. He didn't want to play any mindless games. He decided to accept his alertness and stare at the ceiling above with hopes that he would fall back asleep quickly.

Returning to slumber was not meant to be for John and he began to think backwards from this current moment. He smiled as he thought about the visit from Denise and the kids. He felt pain as he thought about the culture at Hyde Park. He thought through each of his stops and back to his days as an undergraduate, just trying to make sense of it all. He walked so deeply in his journey of reflection that he hardly noticed the nurse enter the room. John complied with each of her requests and politely answered all questions, but he quickly returned to his thoughts. He wandered through the halls of his own history. He remembered who he once was and why he went into education. John remembered the students that he wanted to reach. As he contemplated, the nurse finished her check and softly spoke a polite, "thank you" as she turned out the lights and closed the door. John was alone again, thinking about his life.

John thought of the person he had become and he hated that person. He felt the years of struggle and the weight of the battles he fought. He remembered the person he once wanted to be and realized that through all the accolades and awards, the respect of his colleagues, and the ability to claim victory, it was all temporary. He started to think about the concept of legacy and what that really meant. John started to put the pieces together and the realization came to him. As he recalled the conversation with the parent at West Rock—where he rebutted the expectation that Bill had of his time by saying, "My kids are home right now wondering where their daddy is tonight and why he can't be there to tuck them in"— John started to realize that Bill wanted to see a principal who would be completely invested in the school. He wanted it to be the best possible experience for his kids. For his kids. For his kids! This echoed in John's mind.

This moment of realization opened his eyes to a part of his emptiness and discontent. "My legacy is at home. My legacy is my children. My legacy is in how I love."

As he thought more about the investment Bill was making by doing so much at the school and standing next to him that night as the game, he knew he was doing it all for his kid. Bill was spending the only capital that anyone has in life: time and love. He was spending it in the focus of raising and supporting his son. John's eyes welled up with tears. He could barely see as the water filled his eyes and then, in an instant, the tears flowed effortlessly down his cheeks. All this time, he had been searching for a way to find approval, legacy, revenge, and to make his life worthwhile that he was blind to the most obvious legacy: his family. John continued to reflect on what he hadn't been at home and how little his children knew him and who he was behind the "dad" title. This led John to more questions that would shake his foundation.

The journey of thought led him to questions that he had not revisited in many years. "Who am I? What is important to me? What really matters in this world? What matters in the big picture? What really lasts? How do I want to be remembered when I pass?" John asked these questions over and over again. He wasn't necessarily trying to answer them, he just wanted to deeply understand what he was asking himself.

"Who am I?" seemed to be the most daunting and possibly unanswerable question at the moment, so John decided to skip that one for now. "People have been trying to answer that forever. I need something a bit less cliché," he thought to himself.

"What is important to me?" This question grabbed John's attention. He thought of many possibilities, but through his reflective journey, a theme started to develop. He thought, "If it was all stripped away and I could only live by what I loved, what would those things be?"

Regardless of what his past actions communicated, John loved his family. Denise and the kids were everything to him; they were his heart and soul. That word "soul" touched a nerve with him.

"Faith," he whispered quietly to himself.

John became sullen. He remembered how much he loved God, but that his life spoke little of his faith and how much he loved the Creator. He wondered if his kids knew how important his relationship with God was to him. John worried that they were missing foundation of faith because he wasn't there to teach them the power of love, hope, and trust.

John began to think of his friends Miguel and Tristan and their families. The most dyed-in-the-wool loyal and loving people who enriched his life. In his search for legacy, he gave little effort in the preservation of these relationships. In his self-centric world, John became a friend who made others work for his companionship. He was certain that they must have felt neglected and taken for granted, but he deeply understood their importance in his life and how much he appreciated them. He vowed to be a better friend.

John continued to think of what was important to him. Freedom was at the tip of his tongue. He wanted financial freedom. In his effort to demonstrate his success, John had reached for things—material possessions that served to make others think he was doing well. For him, these things represented his restlessness with his own path. Things that were purchased to fill some type of void only led to greater un-fulfillment as they could not fill the holes he was trying to fill. Then John purchased more and more to fill this continuing void until he had gone into such debt that he was working just to stay afloat.

"So many of us fall into the trap of things being a way to fill our hearts, but in the end they leave us emptier than before. It's as if our souls are grieving, and in order to stop it, we buy ourselves stuff. Our soul recognizes this poor attempt at comfort and it wails with greater pain. The key to freedom is to release myself from the bondage of materialism and debt. Freedom is important to me." John thought as he sighed with shame.

Along with freedom, John believed in the importance of fitness. Living a life filled with stress, he often reached for sugar-laden or processed foods to provide comfort. This led to him gaining a great deal of weight. As his body expanded, his capacities diminished. He felt as though his weight was stealing his functionality and ultimately, his physical freedom as well.

John pressed himself deeper into the question of what is important. Two final answers surfaced. Music was John's lifeblood. He wasn't surprised that there, in the quiet of the night, his mind settled on music as being important to him. For as long as he could remember, he was surrounded by music. He loved it. Music was there for him at every turn in life and it was the voice that understood him within his misunderstood self. John remembered the lyrics he had written and how much he desired to write again. As he thought about it, he realized that it wasn't just music, but the creative expression of writing. John wanted to write and connect his emotions and experiences to paper. In his mind this was limited to lyrics, but this process would open up a door to a new world and a new life.

As the nurse came in again at 2:15 AM, John had spent the last three hours in thought to determine what was important to him. The nurse recognized that he was awake, but she believed that it was due to her arrival. She smiled pleasantly and softly asked to take John's vitals. As he honored the request, he recited what was important in his mind.

"Faith, family, friends, freedom, music, and writing." John said this over and over; he was afraid to forget it. As the nurse left, she turned out the light. John grabbed his phone, activated the flashlight function and wrote this to remember it: 4FMW. He didn't want to wake in the morning without a direct reminder of what his heart and mind found during the night. As he turned off his phone, he started to ponder the question, *"What really matters in this world?"* John drifted off to sleep. The question would resurface again, but for now, rest.

The next day brought a number of visitors to see how John was doing. Friends and colleagues made time out of their day to stop by and check on him. He was touched by each visit and the love that was shared with him. John was grateful to see Katina, Kirk, Miguel, Tristan, and so many others. His phone was buzzing so frequently that he had to turn off the notifications so he could focus on the people in front of him. Messages streamed in throughout the day, and the room became so busy that Denise would read John the message and respond for him. His incredible soreness did not dampen the power of love and kindness that was being gifted to him. As John painfully laughed at jokes and cried with those who were relieved to see him alive, the moments were not lost on him. He felt grateful and positive. The people who were reaching out with genuine kindness were fueling his soul. He decided he would never forget what he was experiencing, and an overwhelming sense of gratitude encompassed John's heart.

That night, as the room was cleared of visitors, Denise and the kids gave John a kiss and wished him a goodnight. "It looks like we may be getting you home tomorrow," Denise said.

It was a major miracle that John survived the crash with only a concussion, a variety of large bruises, and some cuts on his face and hands. His days in the hospital would come to a close tomorrow. He reflected on the events of the day and the questions that filled his head the night before returned.

As darkness engulfed the world outside his room, John was again visited by a nurse. This nurse was a different person than he had seen before. "Hey there John. Welcome to Flo's Shift. We're going to have a marvelous time tonight as I check on you."

John was surprised at this introduction as everyone else had been quiet, but this nurse seemed more commanding of his attention. "What brings you in to see me?" she asked.

John chuckled and said, "I heard that Flo's Shift was an experience not to be missed." He immediately realized what he had just said. Overcome with guilt due to the loss of a life, he hung his head in shame. "Actually, I was in a bad wreck. The other driver didn't survive."

Flo responded sweetly, "I'm sorry John. I truly am."

Flo quickly changed the subject to John's vitals. As she scanned the room, she saw all the cards and remnants of visitors. "Looks like you have a lot of people who care about you."

"I don't know how, but yes, I do," John responded.

"What do you mean by that?" Flo quickly shot back.

"I've spent too much of my life living for my work, I don't know how I've meant anything to most of them. I've never made people the priority they should have been."

Flo responded with hope. "Everyone touches the lives of those around them. Whether you realize it or not, you mean something to the people around you. Too many people go through this world thinking they don't have an impact on others. Just look around you. You are loved. Appreciate it, and stop doubting what you have given to them."

John was dumbfounded by Flo's response. "I guess I never thought about it. I've been so busy trying to do too many things that I didn't see what was going on around me. I mean, I guess I missed the people who care about me. I'm just surprised that they haven't given up on me."

Flo chuckled, "Too many people trying to do too many things in this world. I get quite a few of those patients here. Normally they come see me because of heart attacks or strokes. They rarely return to the person they once were. From the looks of your chart and what I know, you are going to be just fine. Looks like you'll be able to make it up to them. Now, enjoy your night's rest. Looks like you are going home tomorrow. Good night John."

Flo exited the room as quickly as she entered. She was off to the next patient, but John didn't move on. He realized the truth that Flo so quickly pointed out. The questions he had been asking—*"What matters in the big picture? What really lasts? How do I want to be remembered when I pass?"*—seemed to fit so perfectly in his discussion with Flo. The answers were there.

"What matters in the big picture? The impact we have

on people. How we treat them and how we make them feel about themselves. What really lasts? The legacy is how we invest ourselves in others. The love, kindness, hope, and inspiration we share lives on long after we are gone, but this legacy is powerful. How do I want to be remembered when I pass?" John sat silently on this one. He took a moment and then said to himself, "I want to be remembered as being someone who made a difference for others. I want to be remembered as being inspiring, loving, hopeful, and kind." He drifted off to sleep.

John woke in the morning to the sound of shuffling as Denise and the kids came into the room. The discharge papers were signed and an orderly with a wheelchair was on schedule to be there in less than an hour. John told Denise about his conversation with Flo the night before. He told her about Flo's comments and how he was beginning to see things a bit more clearly. Denise smiled. "Let's get you ready to go, but I want to hear all about it when we get home."

CHAPTER TWELVE
KINDNESS

John loved sharing every detail with Denise. He told her all he had thought about and how he changed his focus. "I want to honor those who have always believed in me, but the days of having to be on top are gone. Life is about making a difference for others, not about bottom lines. I have to be the person I was meant to be, nothing more and nothing less. In all of this, I will keep you and the kids as my top priority. It is time for me to make a difference for you."

Denise was overcome with a rush of joy. She shed tears of happiness. "You were never a bad husband or father. You are a great father and a good husband. It's just...I just figured that we had to weather this part of life to get to the other side."

John stopped her. "I love you, but I'm not afraid of the truth. Maybe you believe that I was good enough, but there is so much more I have to give. I can love you and the kids more deeply. I will be the man you didn't know you could dream of." The tears began to subside as great hope took hold. "I believe love is more than a feeling, it is action. I'm going to live this. I can't do it all overnight, but I think I need to start with redefining me and my behaviors. I'm going to focus on one word: kindness."

"That's great John. I love you."

John continued, "I figure there is not enough kindness in the world. If I can work against the grain of the world, I might find a better me at the end—and a better us. I can be a better example for our children. Kindness is key." They spent time that day rehashing some of their conversation, but the best part was they were together, truly together, for the first time in years.

It had been a week since John was at work. His stint in the hospital and time at home allowed him to regroup and truly set his mind in a different state. He spent time every day thinking about "4FMW" and his focus on kindness. He wrote the word down and the kids even made a drawing for him showcasing the word for his office. John knew he was ready for a different path.

John kissed Denise and the kids goodbye and he got into the driver's seat of his rental car, ready to go back to work. His hands began to shake as this was the first time he would drive since the accident. Denise had picked the car up for him, but it sat in the garage for a few days. John's mind was screaming messages of fear to him, but he decided to pray. He prayed for courage, alertness, and safety. He still held guilt for what had taken place, but he put on his sunglasses, his favorite playlist, and he started the car. It seemed like hours before John finally put the car in drive.

His commute was filled with hyper-focused anxiety. Feeling every vibration and seeing every vehicle around him, John was pure driving paranoia. His added cautiousness was creating anger for those who were impacted by his slower-than-the-speed-limit pace. It wasn't long until one of the cars behind him decided to pass, and the driver began honking as if to give him a message about their collective anger and frustration. John backed off the pedal to allow for safer passage. Then a second car began to pass, then another, and another. John pulled up his bootstraps and pressed the pedal closer to the floor. He developed a bit of comfort as the car was traveling at three miles over the speed limit and only one car remained behind him. This car began to pass John as well, and John maintained speed as the driver pulled up beside him. The driver was a younger man with a skinny build.

As John stayed focused forward, the driver beeped. Out of instinct, John looked over and was treated to the visual of a single finger standing at attention. The driver slammed on the gas, cut John off, and hit the brakes hard. John reacted quickly and was able to prevent another accident. The driver sped off and John had a decision to make. He could let his fight take over or, he could act with kindness. He was furious, but—remembering his thoughts in the hospital and the promise he made to Denise—he forced himself to let kindness take over. John used positive self-talk to de-escalate his anger. He used it to regain confidence. In doing so, he found the power to let the situation roll off his back. John found it to be peaceful and empowering.

As he arrived at work, John was ready to go about business as usual. Instead, he would spend the day being blessed by acts of kindness from his coworkers. Normally, this sort of attention would make John uncomfortable, but today was different. He was mindful of how busy they were, yet they were making time to show him care and concern. He took the time to appreciate these moments. He reflected,

"This isn't just a transaction taking place between people. This is a transformative interaction that is teaching me about the power of kindness." John felt curious and blessed.

The day concluded and John began his drive home. Growing traffic interrupted his self-reflection, and John was getting close to being late to pick up the kids from daycare. He began to press the pedal and his mind. Stress started to creep in as he hit a backed up exit ramp and cars who seemed unconcerned with moving forward. With ten minutes remaining until the center closed, John was still a good distance away. The kids were counting on him and as he broke through the logjam of cars, he pushed to make up some time. With less than 2 minutes to close and being less than a mile away, John felt the swell of hope that he would make it just under the wire.

He came to a stretch of road with no one ahead, and John thought he was in the clear. As this thought entered his mind, he saw a car pull out in front of him from a side street. This car pulled out so quickly John thought they would be moving with purpose and he didn't think it would impede his progress. Wrong.

The car was traveling ten miles under the speed limit and John became frustrated. He began to get angry thinking about how they should have let him go by and the driver had no need to be traveling so slowly. As his thoughts became angrier, John realized that the driver in front of him was an elderly woman. "Oh great!" he said to himself, "Perfect timing!" Fortunately, that comment triggered something in his mind. John remembered his morning. He remembered how he felt being pressured to speed up. He thought, "If only people knew what I was going through, maybe they would have cut me some slack." John resumed his focus on the road ahead and the driver in front of him. He had an idea of what she was feeling with an angry driver pressuring her to drive faster. In that moment his perspective changed. He began to think, "How did I want those drivers to react me this morning? Kindness," John said aloud. He backed off the other car, backed off his speed. He was at peace with his reaction; he felt good. As John looked to the right, he noticed a police car monitoring traffic. He had just experienced a rare thing: an immediate benefit to practicing kindness. John was convinced that there was more to kindness than he was seeing, but he was thankful for what he did know: it is transformational.

John showed up late to pick up the kids, but he was at peace with being late for the sake of kindness. He decided that whatever financial penalty he would have to pay was worth it. John walked in and the kids were having a blast with other children who had parents stuck in traffic. The director of the center told him not to worry about being late as several parents were impacted by a variety of traffic situations. Kindness paid off again.

CHAPTER THIRTEEN
FOUR MEN DISCUSS

As John continued to practice kindness as a daily and life-changing endeavor, he noticed his focus was changing. People started to matter more than ever, especially his friends. Over the years, John had two friends who stayed by his side with no conditions. Although he gave them little priority during his years spent climbing the ladder of success, Miguel and Tristan stuck with him. They waited for their friend to return to the person they knew existed under the hard-driving legacy seeker.

Miguel and Tristan were unique in their way of living. Filled with love and positivity, they were loyal to the core. Their families and John's family grew together in size and connectedness. They relied on each other and as John wandered in focused determination to make his life count, the bonds between their wives and children grew stronger. As he reconnected with his friends, they came to the realization that they were a family who happened to also be friends.

John was always loyal to his friends in word and support, but he realized that throughout the years he consistently short-changed them on his time. He needed to invest further in these relationships that spanned several years. They were important to him. John's friends were true to the core and he wanted to return the same level of commitment. He wanted to share how he felt about Tristan and Miguel; he wanted them to know they were like brothers to him and that he loved them. John had no idea how to say any of this. His former self was still battling within him, whispering all the negative and fear-based things one can say. This former self challenged John's toughness, his masculinity, and his capacity to change. That former self may have hidden from the power of John's recent realizations and his efforts to recalibrate his priorities, but it ambushed him on several concepts, this being one of them. He struggled with vulnerability.

John thought to himself, "I don't know how to even approach this with the two of them. It's too uncomfortable. After all, Miguel isn't touchy-feely and Tristan would wonder where the hell all this was coming from. It's too weird. I'll just leave it be." John was pulling into a coffee shop and his former self was putting the finishing touches on burying his desire to express what he felt was important to be shared.

As he walked in, he heard the conversation. Four men discussing love, its virtues, and implications. The owner of the coffee shop stood off to the side, listening, but not participating. The men discussed the concept of love for a few minutes until the oldest of the group spoke with a commanding tone that forced everyone, including John, to listen. "I can't believe that four men are discussing love on a Friday night. Have we nothing better to talk about? What's wrong with us?"

Without hesitation, the coffee shop owner retorted, "More like what's right with you. Is there anything more meaningful and powerful to discuss than love? You chastise yourself and the others as if you were doing something wrong in talking about love. There is nothing more powerful. And unfortunately, I guarantee you that at this moment there are four men somewhere discussing hate and not one of them sees anything wrong with the negativity and destructiveness that is coming from their mouths. Keep discussing love. Be proud of it." The group sat in stunned silence, as did John. He began to reflect.

"Why have we stigmatized love as a trite emotion so that it has become this cheesy 'girlie' feeling that 'real men' can't identify with as valuable and substantive? What have we done to the most powerful and inspiring of emotions?" John began to think, realizing that modern society and cultural stereotypes have attempted to systematically and incrementally turn love into a four-letter word. "What we are dealing with is the devaluation and distortion of love," he thought to himself.

"While our cameras and minds are constantly transfixed on hate, bitterness, and negativity, love has become boring, trite, and scary. When we think of love, we picture candy hearts, momentary feelings that lead to a physical collision, vapid insincerity, and some ethereal concept that has no real place in the practical world. In reality, love is the greatest power that humanity has and at its core is realness, integrity, loyalty, and all the positive energy needed to overcome and heal. Love means that you display it with action. Love isn't just a feeling or word; it is action. It is the impetus of kindness, the genesis of sacrifice, and the foundation of trust. To bring greater love into this world is to begin to address the complex problems that we consistently face. It is the process by which we will begin to heal ourselves. Its vulnerability is key to establishing a legacy that is real and gives to people. Love doesn't require anyone to get credit, but it requires action and vulnerability. Love is the answer."

John continued revealing the weakness of his former self. "I need to love on a greater basis, person to person in a daily walk to become the person I want to be. I have shied away from being overtly loving and I've used sarcastic humor and busting chops to veil the expression of love that so many needed. I have failed in love, but I won't quit and I will grow. I will begin to carry love to those I get to share my life with, whether it is for a moment or for years. This can only be done one interaction at a time." John sat for a while longer and drank the rest of his coffee.

As he walked out the door, the men were re-engaged in their conversation about love. John heard one of the four men supporting the earlier comment of the shop owner, "Without love, nothing great can take place. Without love, there is no hope. If I have faith that can move mountains, but do not have love, I am and have nothing." John was determined to reverse course and let his friends know exactly how he felt about them.

CHAPTER FOURTEEN
COMING HOME

As John opened his heart more, he found he began attracting more people who needed a dose of kindness. He started to see opportunities open for him professionally and a chance to change jobs presented itself. This job was not a path to the superintendency, but a chance to support the work of teachers, secretaries, custodians, bus drivers, and principals. It was not a glamorous role, but it allowed him to serve. The opportunity would ultimately allow John to work in the school district where he lived, so he would get to work on supporting the education of his children. John went for it as it aligned to his recalibrated beliefs.

He was grateful to get the job. His excitement would barely hold until dinner. After they said grace, John looked at his dear children, Jules, Isabel, and Finn, and said, "Daddy's coming home." Jules and Isabel were so thankful they shouted with joy and Denise smiled brighter and bigger than he had seen in a long time. Finn, well…Finn asked a lot of questions. John was happy to answer them all. John, realizing that he had released his dream of making his life count by being "the leader" or searching for respect in a position, found peace in his new quest and his recalibrated self.

Finding his way around his new job and new co-workers was not difficult for John. He was determined to be genuine in every way possible; he didn't want to pretend anymore. He had no desire to play the political game. John was going to make it on the strength of his character, the merit of his ideas, and how he supported others.

John was surrounded by amazing people and he found himself being transformed by their positive mentality and beliefs. His former self battled back early on in his new job, but surrounded by so many positive and genuine people, that old identity began to die of starvation. Among this new group of people, no one caught John's attention more than Grace. Grace was a different soul. The light that generated through her person, actions, and words impacted those around her. No one had a better reputation. John began to realize that Grace was more than a colleague and friend. She had a special role in this world. Grace was a bearer of light.

With nothing feeding his negativity, no enemies to fight within, and a focus on kindness and love, John started to grow strong. The old John was feeling the flames at his feet, as the new John was preparing for an epic transformation. John didn't know what was coming. He just went about his work and continued his focus on serving others.

CHAPTER FIFTEEN
INSPIRE

With John becoming a more positive person, he became more open to advice, perspectives, and inspirational concepts. Whether through quotes, books, podcasts, or videos, he was surrounded by inspiration and saw how it drove the energy of those around him. Grace, Miguel, and Tristan seemed to feed off of this stuff on a daily basis. John became open to what it could do for him and how could it impact his current journey.

In the past, John would have dismissed all of it as a waste of time with little to no practical application. When he received the emailed quote from Reuben so long ago, John appreciated its significance and meaning, but it was treated more like a gift. However, this was a different John. He became curious.

Grace was consistently telling John, "Words matter. That is why I surround myself with words that give me strength, courage, and keep me focused on the big picture." John would think about this concept often. His children's artwork was filled with words such as, peace, love, hope, family, and other positive thoughts. He was wondering if his kids knew something he didn't. He wondered if Grace and his kids were on the same wavelength. A purer line of thought, maybe more innocent and naive, but more powerful, purposeful, and real.

John started consuming inspiration little by little. He started with quotes. His favorites would make the wall in his office, home, or on social media:

"Our greatest glory is not in never falling, but in rising every time we fall."

- Confucius

"It's all secretly perfect."

- Anonymous

"Why fit in when you were born to stand out?"

- Dr. Seuss

"Everyone you meet is fighting a battle you know nothing about. Be kind."

- Anonymous

These quotes seemed to mean something to John, even if he didn't get their depth. They propelled his being when things were tough and their impact made him more curious about the power of words. He reflected and wondered about their deeper applications in his life. John was getting close.

The energy gained from purposeful and positive words became tangible to him. He kept hearing about how books have changed the game for his friends; they all talked about books like *The Radical Leap* by Steve Farber, *The Element* by Sir Ken Robinson, *The Carpenter* by Jon Gordon, *Fully Charged* by Tom Rath, and *The Alchemist* by Paulo Coehlo. John wasn't excited at the thought of reading anything longer than an article. In fact, he was downright agitated at the fact that he kept hearing about books. He didn't feel as though he could sacrifice the time to read. Couple that obstacle with the personal irritation that John was a slow reader and reading seemed like a chore.

John finally confessed his irritation to Grace one afternoon over lunch. With a puzzled look, Grace asked a question. "Why?"

"I hate reading, pure and simple. I used to like it, but now it just takes too long and I can't waste the time."

"OK, you said you used to like it. When was that?" Grace's inquisitive nature and passion for books required her to push the envelope on this subject.

"When I was in elementary school. I couldn't read enough, I loved it. My appetite for books could not be satisfied. Then I hit fourth grade."

"Wait, what happened in fourth grade, John?"

John sighed. "In fourth grade, it lost all of its luster. That was the year we started counting books. It wasn't about learning, enjoying, or anything other than stuffing certain books down my throat to get to a magic number. But it didn't stop with that one year, it continued through middle school and high school. Being told what to read each and every year, being assigned a multitude of pages or chapters each night, it was no longer enjoyable. It was torture. I remember having to read these books deemed as classics by my teachers. The books may have been well written, but they didn't connect with me. Add in the issue of my reading speed and when I attempted to read, it would consume my entire night. In the end, my friend Cliff got me through the misery of reading and school."

"Cliff?" Grace asked.

"You know, Cliff and his notes," John laughed. "Their love for certain books and the idea of making us read at break neck speed killed my love for reading."

"John, that's because you never had me as a teacher. It's all about finding the right book for you. It's that connection and that time to reflect on what the book is saying that makes all the difference. Books allow us to have a richer perspective. Why don't you just pick one book and if you don't like it, stop reading it. I bet you would love *The Alchemist*." Grace was energized.

"I've heard of that book, but I don't know. Let me figure out what I might like to dive into. I'll give this a try, but if I don't like it, will you stop asking me to read?" Reluctantly, Grace agreed.

John took his time finding a book that would seem to work for him. Every day Grace would ask the status of his pick and John would confess he hadn't found one yet. Finally, John went with Grace's original recommendation and picked *The Alchemist* by Paulo Coehlo. He began to read the opening pages, but put it down soon after. John walked away. He read another page or two before bed and laughed to himself knowing that he could finally get Grace to stop asking if he had found a book.

It was 5:00 AM and John woke to a loud thunder clap. The rain on the roof sounded like a stampede as he became more alert. John was over an hour away from his alarm's usual time and didn't feel like getting out of bed. The book was staring at him. John cracked it open one more time. On page 11, a strange feeling came over him. He was not only enjoying what he was reading, but it was also causing him to think about his own life. It was sparking reflection and providing inspiration through the actions of the characters. John was being fueled. When the alarm sounded at 6:15 AM, he was so deeply engrossed with the book that he became irritated at having to put it down. Begrudgingly, he rose from his bed and stepped to the floor. John entered the shower thinking about the story and how it had hooked him.

In the mindless routine of showering, he had thoughts about the book's possible endings and how it caused him to have an internal conversation that expanded his mind. He marveled at the power of sharing a perspective through a story. He realized the power of reading and writing.

John dressed and walked down the staircase to breakfast. On his way, be remembered a story regarding Malcolm X. A rather arrogant person asked Malcolm what university he attended, knowing that he hadn't. The question was obviously asked in an attempt to humiliate and devalue Malcolm, but his response was powerful. "I studied at the University of Books," was Malcolm's response. Powerful and succinct. John wondered if the University of Books was ready for him. What learning could he get and what inspiration could he find in the pages of the literary options that would fuel him to push to the next level?

John began to read as much as possible. Vacations were filled with books and weekends were the blessed times that allowed for reading and reflection. He read whatever he could get his hands on. John didn't know it, but the inspiration he was receiving from his friends and his readings were doing more than sparking a thought process—he was gaining wisdom. He was communing with the heart and soul of the writer to grow.

Through this inspiration, John gained a great deal of knowledge about a world that held possibilities, one that rose above the cynicism and systems that held people in place. Ironically, this world was always there, but he was so steeped in negativity and cynicism, he couldn't see it—he was asleep. John learned about the interconnectedness of all of God's creations, the power of the universe, and the laws God put into place that many ignore. He realized that he wasn't a single being walking separately on this planet, but one that was tied more to the Creator and His creation than he ever dreamed.

John learned a very important part of the human experience—the ripple of influence. Each action we take and each word we speak has an impact on the greater world. Those who are closer to us feel a stronger ripple than those further away, but we all feel it. Where each action and word is a stone landing in the water, the ripples in the water represent the impact it has on those in this world. Our impact and ripples can serve to sink them or raise their perspective and view.

CHAPTER SIXTEEN
AWAKEN

It was early January and John was trying to find a word of focus for the year. The influence of every bit of inspiration was causing his soul and mind to percolate with ideas. John thought, "What could follow kindness?" Love seemed like a natural follow up, but it didn't quite fit him. He began to realize that his drifting in life was almost over and he was setting forth on a journey, but what did he need to do next?

"Maybe…faith." John was excited at this prospect. Faith seemed right for him. He was pleased with himself, with this choice, and he felt as if he could mark the task of picking a word for the year complete. However, John's inner voice wasn't so easily convinced, but he wanted to have his word settled. He wanted it in his time, not God's time.

As John walked the halls of work, he forced faith to the forefront of his mind. A great word for anyone to focus on, but it seemed artificial. John was stubborn and he wanted to move forward, not haggle with himself over this word for weeks. In a discussion with a large group of co-workers, John's boss discussed how faith was his word for the previous year and he was curious to hear what others had chosen. John was smacked with this information. "Do I keep my word? Do I keep looking? I don't want to reject a word, because my boss had it, but I don't want to look like I'm kissing up either." John was uncomfortable and unsettled in knowing that he had to keep looking. This was a sign that he needed some originality; he needed something that was more fitting for him. He heard the little voice inside of him pressing him to go further. He ignored it before, but John had to listen now. He reopened his search for a word with significance.

While John continued to wonder about his course of action, he felt as though he was struggling with himself. He began to reflect on the past few years. He remembered his internal pain and sorrow as he achieved at the highest level and the pain of failure to find fulfillment although the world told him he was successful and whole. John thought of the move to get closer to home and the car crash that would shake his world. He remembered how kindness had impacted him and how much he was changing inside. Then it started to come to him in this time of reflection, "Maybe rebirth. No, that's not it. Maybe renaissance...No! Too pretentious. Maybe it should be realization."

John could feel it. As he stared into the sky, the sun was rising; God's canvas was brilliant. The reds, pinks, black, and blues were amazing and especially vibrant this morning. His heart felt filled with hope. He felt awake for the first time in years. "Awaken," John said with confidence. The word was given to him in God's time. John knew this year he had to focus on his awakening. He didn't quite know what that meant, but he knew it was his focus. It felt right. Through a lightning bolt of natural inspiration, he received his word.

John walked into the office thankful for his progress. His word for the year was set and he felt it was going to be a big year. He saw his journey coming into focus as if one step at a time. As John's day was beginning to get away from him and the flow of the day was speeding up, Grace walked into the office. "Hey John! So good to see you today."

"Good morning Grace, it's good to be seen." John chuckled and followed with, "It's great to see you too." They engaged in one of John's least favorite activities—small talk—but with Grace, John knew it was sincere. Her sincerity enabled him to set his mind and truly engage with the conversation. They talked about so much as their friendship was deepening. He began to rely on Grace's perspective and ability to practice gratefulness on a daily basis. She would often talk about how if a person is grateful, it keeps them from negative emotions and actions. It's through these emotions and actions that a person can cause damage to themselves and their relationships. John, in his weakest moments, used her example to draw strength. He knew what she was sharing was true.

The conversation continued and Grace shared her gratefulness for an amazing sunrise that morning. "I saw it too! And it gave me something I've been searching for these past two weeks. I've got my word."

John revisited his thankfulness for what he had been given. Grace's friendship was rubbing off on John and he was enjoying the changes. He began to tell Grace the story behind his word and he became increasingly animated. When the story peaked, John revealed "awaken" to Grace and her face dropped in astonishment.

"John. I need to tell you something. Today was an unusual morning. I did all the normal things and got ready for work, but when I went to put on my bracelet something wasn't quite right. I had to change it." Grace's love for words was evident. She surrounded herself with positivity and inspiration at home and work. She even had a charm bracelet that allowed her to change letters to make different words. Grace revealed to John her bracelet. The word awake stared back at him.

"John, I put the word 'aware' on the bracelet this morning, but it didn't feel right. I don't know why I had to change it, but I saw the letter K in the drawer and thought I needed to change the 'aware' to 'awake.'" Grace began laughing with excitement. John was dumbfounded and filled with a mysterious wonder. It was if he was being sent a sign.

"That's silly," he thought. "Signs aren't real, right?" John kept the internal dialogue to himself, but it puzzled him. He stared at Grace's bracelet and a mist came to his eyes. He felt special; he wanted to believe that God was talking to him. John was waking up. Grace gave John a hug and continued in her excitement. John was appreciative but stunned.

As the tyranny of time rests for no one, John and Grace's moment was interrupted by a co-worker, "John don't be late to the meeting." John gathered his things, hugged Grace again, and hustled off to the next meeting on his schedule. The bracelet and that morning would stick in John's thoughts and he would reflect on it frequently. God was talking, but was John aware and listening?

As the year progressed, John became more receptive to thoughts that challenged his viewpoints. He started to become acutely aware that people were living in different worlds on this planet. He observed the role of fear and hope, doubt and belief, as well as ambiguity and purpose in the lives of those around him.

He started to wonder what was behind the victory and unlikely successes of people in the world. Over the years, John had witnessed many people take a leap in life and experience great failure that was often followed by greater success. He knew that Grace had insights on this and he craved the discussion. He set weekly lunch meetings to discuss projects for work, but also to dive deeper into the unseen reality of life.

During one of these meetings, John and Grace were discussing the great ideas that were taking shape in the district. They talked about how certain educators made a tremendous difference for their students. Grace pointed out the tremendous growth some of their young teachers were demonstrating and this allowed John to transition to the conversation he really wanted to have. "Grace, I can't put my finger on it, but I believe something greater is behind the success of people who find their place in this world. We know that success—real success that matters—can be found somewhere in the true knowledge of the concepts of hope, belief, and purpose."

Grace responded with a question, "Have you ever heard of abundance and scarcity thinking?"

"No, but tell me more," John replied.

"Well, the world lives within these two mindsets. Scarcity being the belief that there is only so much to go around of any and everything; capabilities, emotions, purpose, health, resources, and so on. In this mindset, the person traps themselves with the fear that they are only capable of doing or getting so much out of life. Fear rules the person in this mindset. This person struggles with the success of others believing that it will impact their potential for success. This creates strong negative feelings and these feelings are often what hold people back from achieving their dreams and purpose. Remember when we talked about how negative emotions and actions end up hurting the person feeling or acting on them? This is prevalent in scarcity thinking. Ultimately, fear prevents us from taking the leap to being all we were meant to be in life.

"However, an abundance mindset is the opposite. People who live in abundance believe that there is plenty to go around. They believe that we can develop ourselves to meet challenges and there is a deep belief in one's personal worth. Abundance mindset leads to enjoying the good that happens to others. It breeds positivity, gratitude, and success. Gratitude is the key." As Grace finished her abridged version of this concept, she could see the wheels turning in John's mind. He was intrigued.

Grace continued, "Couple the abundance mindset with the Law of Attraction and you have a powerful combination that the most successful people attribute to being the secret to their success."

John furrowed his brow. "Law of Attraction? I'm not sure if I ever heard of that before."

"That's a bigger discussion, but to simplify it, the law of attraction is understanding that everyone emits energy through their thoughts and mindset. This energy can be haphazard and negative, therefore drawing in negative circumstances and situations; or it can be intentional and positive, thus drawing in positive circumstances and situations. It is up to the person to visualize and put into the universe the things they want and are willing to work towards. The universe finds a way to bring it to you. Whatever your heart is putting out, it will attract that same in return. It's the Law of Attraction coupled with the power of intentional thought."

"But what if you don't know what you want out of life?" John sheepishly asked.

"You need to find it. John, we're all created to serve a greater purpose. We weren't made the same. We all have different gifts. When we use these gifts, we compliment each other. We add to the lives of those around us. Our gifts were given to us so we can serve God by investing in each other. You have gifts and a purpose, you just don't know what it is yet. However, when you do know, you will see things differently and your life will rise to a different plane. You will leave the distraction of the moment and your heart will expand to meet the requirements of your purpose. Then you will know what you want out of life."

John struggled with Grace's words as they cut to the heart and he remembered how his path in life was once driven by a legacy with no purpose. He was unaware of his gifts. John knew that he had a good personality; he knew he was funny, but he truly didn't know what he brought to the table. "Grace, I don't know who I really am. I don't know why I am here. I do know that I've been forcing myself into so many boxes and molds along the way to try and figure it out, but this has led me to places where I haven't completely fit. I've found hollowness when I became what the world wanted me to become.

What do I do? How can I find what I am supposed to do and be?" John was becoming desperate.

"That's between you and God. You need to listen," Grace responded.

"You mean to pray?" John asked.

"No, John. God is always talking. You have been too busy working and hustling to listen. You hear what is being said, but you often resist it. He doesn't need you to talk. He wants you to begin to listen. God is always talking. It is up to us to get quiet and listen."

"What do you mean Grace? How is God talking?"

Grace gently looked at John with sympathy. "The signs are everywhere John. God speaks to us through people, signs, and situations. He opens up the universe to communicate with us. You have to start noticing and recognizing. See the signs. Hear those around you. Learn from the situations. Hear what the universe is trying to tell you."

With that statement Grace gave John a hug and had to leave. "I have to observe a new teacher in 10 minutes and I can't be late. Just listen. His universe is talking." Grace left and John was quiet.

John sat silent for a few minutes, but a mountain of email was screaming to be addressed and he had phone messages to return. John tried to bury his thoughts in the work. He hoped for the blissful ignorance of distraction, but the universe was calling for his attention. He strained to focus on the tasks in front of him. He did the best he could, but John was in a run-out-the-clock situation. He worked to pass the time, as the clock approached the end of the work day, John was feeling a call to drive.

The bustling offices where John worked had slowed to barely

a crawl when he gathered his things to leave for the weekend. His conversation with Grace was still weighing heavy on his mind. He didn't know where to start, but he knew he had to start somewhere.

John called Denise as he got into the car. He told her about the conversation with Grace and was hoping that Denise would counter the concepts that Grace shared. Much to John's dismay, Denise pushed him further. "What are you really about John?" she asked. "What really makes it all worthwhile? What adds to you?"

"If I knew that, I wouldn't be talking about this, I would be doing it." John was irritated in not receiving the relief he was hoping for from Denise.

"You'll find it. I know you will. Start listening," she said.

"I think I need to drive. Are you OK with picking up the kids? I'm not sure how late I will be."

"I got this, babe. Just do what you need to do," Denise said.

John was at the cusp. A new world of reality. A possibility of a new and deeper life. The flames of new thinking and challenges were engulfing John's person. As the old John was turning to ash, a new John was coming into being. John was a phoenix about to rise from his ashes.

CHAPTER SEVENTEEN
THE SHERPA

John hung up the phone with the road calling for his attention. John loved to drive and think, even after his initial reservations about driving again following his accident. He loved the music that would surround him on the road. John was an eclectic music enthusiast and listened to a variety of genres and artists. He had a talent for putting together the most unusual playlists. They would puzzle his friends and co-workers, but the mix of music often soothed his scattered thought processes. John had a special playlist for an occasion like this. "The Sherpa" would take him on a journey and accompany him in his deepest thoughts. A mix of artists that was headlined by Rush, John Mayer, Mumford and Sons, John Butler, Alicia Keys, Alanis Morissette, Jimi Hendrix, and Miles Davis to name a few. John had the volume turned up and the windows down as he headed down a country road. His reflection began.

"What are my gifts? What is my purpose?" he asked repeatedly. He was frustrating himself with his lack of a viable response. John remembered that God and His universe were always talking. He stayed in that line of thought until he came to a stop sign, where, across from him, he saw a large white sign with huge black lettering. "The Abundant Church" was plastered in bold, man-sized font to gain the eyes of anyone traveling by.

John sat at the stop sign to read the words closely. Underneath "The Abundant Church" was a Bible verse. Proverbs 18:16, "A man's gift makes room for him, and brings him before great men." The conflict of emotions was like a wrestling match as John struggled between excitement, skepticism, and anxiety.

"The universe is talking", he thought. "What is my gift? I keep asking that and I don't feel like I'm figuring it out." John kept driving and he continued to struggle. His brain was growing weary in thought and he began to hope for distraction. He wanted to give up his drive and he thought of going home.

John was petrified that Grace might be wrong. He was terrified that he had nothing of worth to give to this world. He turned up the music. Alanis was in an indignant mood as she sang, "All I Really Want." John attempted to drown his thoughts as she sang the words, "Why are you so petrified of silence? Here can you handle this?" The music cut out for two seconds. Alanis returns as John remains quiet. She asks, "Did you think about your bills, your ex, your deadlines, or when you think you're gonna die? Or did you long for the next distraction?"

The universe spoke again. John was beyond it. This felt unfair. He only wanted to figure out what God wanted him to do. He just wanted to have a purpose. "I keep hearing from the universe, but it's not giving me any answers!"

John started to become emotional. He flashed like a strobe

light between anger, anxiousness, fear, and frustration. He pulled the car off the road and into a park. Dusk was about to fall and the park was deserted. John left the driver's seat and began to walk towards a bench by a wooded area, internal dialogue filled with conflict. He was feeling tortured by the signs that the universe was sending his way. He wondered if God was playing a cruel joke on him as frustration and anger filled his eyes. John desperately wanted distraction. Like an addict looking for an emotional escape, John reached for his phone and social media.

When the universe is talking and you are aware that it's calling your name, its power can overtake any distraction. John saw a video of a television host at the end of his show addressing the audience. The host, Steve Harvey, was known for his intense wit and ability to draw out uncontrollable laughter. John believed it would be great viewing as he desperately needed a laugh. He wanted to take his mind off of gifts and purpose. He wanted to stop thinking about the universe. But the universe wasn't done talking to John.

Steve began, "I'm going to share something with you. I'm going to tell you something that every successful person has to do. Believe it or not. Including you." John was preparing for a punch line. He listened closely.

Steve continued, "Every successful person in this world has jumped." He went on to explain that if someone is waking up thinking that there is more to their life, they are just existing. He expressed the importance of believing that there is more, but in order to get to that life, a person has to jump. When God created us, he gave us all gifts. It is more than running, jumping, singing, and dancing. It can be networking, connecting the dots, teaching, baking pie, or cutting grass. John felt betrayed by Steve, but he was still listening.

"I have a partner who loves cutting grass and his landscaping company makes 4 million dollars a year. Just cutting grass. That's his gift." Steve continued to say that when you go to the edge of the cliff of life and see people soaring by, and you think, how are they doing that? Have you ever thought that maybe they have identified their gift and they are living in it? You can get an education and that's nice, but if you don't use your gift, your education can only take you so far. Steve said that the gift is what provides the soar. If you are going to a job that you don't like, you aren't living. You're just existing. You need to try living. As the video was nearing the end, John heard that when you jump off that cliff of life and use your gift, you will crash and get scraped up. But as long as you maintain the courage to use your gift and keep jumping, at some point that gift will open up and provide you with the soar.

Steve quoted the verse John read on the church sign, "Your gift will make room for you." Then, he quoted John 10:10: "He comes to give you life and give it to you more abundantly." Steve recognized and stated a critical point. "That is a promise of God. That ain't a theory; that's a promise." His words hit home. John knew that none of this was a coincidence. God was using His universe to talk to him. He settled himself. John knew who was talking.

As darkness fell across the park, John made it back to his car. His heart told him that it was time to stop being anything other than himself. He realized that if he wanted to find his gifts, he had to get to the edge of the cliff of life and jump.

Because of fear, John hid himself and what he loved for so long. He didn't know how it fit in his world. He was fearful of what people would say and if they would see any value in what he loved. He didn't want to be an impostor or fraud, but he was ready to pull back the curtains that covered who he was, what he really loved, and what he really desired. John was ready to get scraped up and feel life. He wanted to live. John was ready to be vulnerable and real.

John loved music. He loved creativity. He loved being different and he believed in the spiritual mysteries of life. He saw a different picture of the world and the life it supported. He spent the rest of the drive home thinking about how he could strip away all the stuff of society and the lies he accepted for so many years.

John was focused on getting to the heart of the matter. He felt he wanted to be a songwriter. Only one problem, though: John still didn't know anything about musical theory, notes, or processes. He just knew he heard the song in his head and the lyrics flowed quickly and fluently. John had to figure out if there was any substance to this. "Screw possibility or rationality. Forget being realistic. If this means I live my life poor and happy so be it, but I have to try and see where this goes. I want to try living."

John pulled into the garage and he looked at all the tools, toys, bikes, and things that accumulated and lived in this part of his home. "All of this doesn't matter. What if it was gone tomorrow? We would survive. We would be fine. What if I didn't have this house, these cars, cable television, internet, all this stuff. It doesn't make us happy. It's more clutter in our lives. We can't take it with us anyway," John's thoughts seemingly referenced doom, but he was simply thinking about the fragile nature of life.

"What if I knew when my time would come? What would I do with my life?" This common thought gave way to an idea—an idea that would help get John to take the next step in finding his gifts and purpose. "What if I had a year to live and the only way to add years to my life was to do the one thing that my heart desired? What would it be?" John's thoughts were finally giving him perspective. It didn't take him long to think about what that would be. The universe led him to the place he wanted to go, it just didn't happen in John's timing. It happened in God's timing.

John decided to take a step to the cliff of life and begin the honest journey to find who he was and what he was here to do.

CHAPTER EIGHTEEN
SEEK

John slept soundly through the night. He discovered that the time spent reflecting and being in one's own mind was an exhausting, but fulfilling process.

He opened his eyes and immediately, his belief in the interconnectedness of people was on his mind. He learned through the process of being inspired that we can make an impact on those around us through our ripple of influence. He believed that finding his gift and purpose was critical to himself, but also to those who were within that ripple.

With his new outlook and newfound bravery, John decided to push his own limits. He decided to revisit the question and answer he slept on last night. "What would I do if I only had a year to live, but could add years if I did what my heart desired? I would write songs and perform," John thought. Then he asked himself a follow-up question. "Why? What purpose does it serve to the world, the people in my ripple of influence?" John's reflection led him down the path of his previous songwriting and his reason for starting in education.

Although John's songs generally followed the love route, he really wanted to create songs that were inspirational and contained some philosophical substance. He wanted to encourage people to dig deep into their lives and find inspiration. He remembered that he wanted to be the ladder that people used to see above their current life and to dream of the possibilities that lay before them. He wanted to be the one who said "You Can" in a sea of doubters and cynical thinkers. John wanted his music to be inspiring.

There is great power in inspiration and John knew it. "If I can inspire people to stop existing and to start living, while gaining insight into the unique and powerful beings that we are, maybe, just maybe we can change this world," he thought. John shuddered with disbelief in what he was saying. "The world? I think I'm overestimating my ripple effect." He knew he was on to something, but needed to stay humble.

His teenage years taught him that not practicing humility had its severe consequences. John was hyper-vigilant against the infection of outward pride and arrogance. He worked to keep himself in check, even to the detriment of his potential purpose and devaluing his own amazingness. John felt that he must aim for a lesser goal than "the world," so he settled on those around him and hoped to have the opportunity to someday impact his region, state and, in a greater fantasy, his country.

John was excited at his prospects of inspiring people through music. He began to wonder how this could happen.

One evening John was working late. He had a major project coming up and needed to burn the candle at both ends to make things happen. He enjoyed his work of breaking the mold for schools because he wanted to leave the dull, one-size-fits-all approach and find a better way to meet needs while empowering through choice. This was his passion project for the district he served.

John needed a mental break from the late night grind and he decided to spend some time watching inspiring and thought-provoking videos. He came across videos on many topics: introversion by Susan Cain, vulnerability by Brene Brown, and knowing the why by Simon Sinek. The links of these talks led to others and eventually, to Oprah's Soulful Sunday series with Brene Brown, Mark Nepo, and more. John was swallowing the information as if it were water to a parched desert traveler. Before he realized it, it had been almost an hour and he had to get back to the project. John saw one last link and gave himself permission to click one last time.

It was a simple link to Megan Macedo's website that was titled, "Be Yourself, Tell Your Story, Do Something that Matters." Megan spoke in a captivating and individual way. It seemed as if she was right there talking to John directly.

Megan said, "We spent so many years conforming to how we think we are supposed to be, that whenever you realize that you can do it your own way, it takes time to distill what's really us. Common wisdom says that failure is our greatest fear, but I think what we are most afraid of is the scale of our own ambition. And over the years, through fear, we've disconnected from that part of our self that wants to be someone who leaves a trace.

We don't often tell anyone else about our fantasies of success and impact, but they're there. At times, I would deny my big dreams and tell myself that the mature thing to do is to accept that it's not possible and that life's full of compromise. A compromise is necessary in life, but not that kind."

John reflected on the compromise that he made with himself and the realization that it would take time to find himself fully. He made two promises that day to himself:

1. He promised that he wouldn't compromise on his purpose or his dream. John wanted to inspire the world and would accept nothing less. John said to himself, "There is no plan B. I will be used to inspire the world with my gifts. That's why I am here."

2. John promised that he would allow a process to take place and he would be open to that process. "No more resisting and being impatient," he said. "I will let God and His universe take me on a journey to discover the 'what' and the 'how.'"

John held a realization that the available, the unlikely, and the broken are used by God to do great things. He believed that if something is broken and unlikely—but available—and they do great things, there is only one reason: God. If someone is seemingly perfect and likely, they get the credit.

John said to himself, "I want the world to see the power of God through my life and what God has given me. I don't know how this will happen, but I don't have to worry about that. I only have to focus on this journey to share the gifts I have and to let God show the path one step at a time." His heart was warm and full. At the corner of his desk sat a journal Grace had purchased for him as a gift. Its cover had a message to John. "Have The Courage To Dream" was set boldly in gold.

He opened its blank pages of new possibility for the first time.

Inside the cover he read, "Dream without Fear, Love without Limits." John finally decided to contribute what was in his heart. He wrote, "Dream Big" inside the cover, which was something he heard from Miguel and Tristan quite often and "Use the talents God gave you! Share them with others!" on the top of the first page. John was broken, he was unlikely, but now he became available to God.

John stepped forward with what he thought was his gift—music. He began to share his lyrics with musicians that he knew. John wanted to get feedback and some validation that what he wrote wasn't self-deluded garbage, so he sang the songs in quiet, private forums. In each instance, the feedback was overwhelmingly positive and encouraging. They believed that the lyrics and melody John had shared was worth developing.

However, with each opportunity, John was becoming increasingly aware that his voice wasn't quite right. His karaoke abilities to entertain were off the charts outstanding, but this wasn't a joke. This was his heart on the line. John felt that maybe his path was to find a singer who would sing his songs and a musician who could write the melodies in his mind. John wondered if God wanted him to be a lyricist.

John worked diligently at understanding music and its processes. The natural match to the power of music was evident, but the fit with writing the notes wasn't there. John, citing the work of Steven Pressfield in his book, *The War of Art*, was determined that this was just a part of the learning process and resistance to his path. He continued to share his work, and with the continued validation from the music professionals he knew, John stepped out further to the edge of the cliff. He shared more of his songs on paper. He shared them with some friends, Denise, and at a poetry reading. The responses were all positive, but he knew something was missing.

Several days later, John's lunch meeting with Grace was drawing to a close. Their plans for the week were set and as the server left the bills at the table, John reached into his backpack. "Grace, I need to share something with you and I want- no, I need your honest opinion." Grace became excited at the veiled surprise. John revealed a notebook and told Grace what she would find inside. "I think this is the key to my gifts. Here are the songs I have been writing on and off since I was young."

Grace was delighted at the opportunity to see John's heart and creativity on paper. She gladly took the notebook and John directed her to his most recent works. He waited in nervous anticipation. He knew Grace's wonderful and supportive nature would not allow for harsh criticism, but John also knew her well enough to see the signs when things aren't quite right. Grace read and turned the page, then another, and another.

John sat in anticipatory silence. Grace's eyes lifted from the page. She had an unfamiliar look. She was silent for a moment, then she took a breath.

"Wow! You are a writer!"

John blushed and responded, "Come on, Grace. You're too kind. Do you really think they're good?"

Grace leaned in and grabbed John's hand. She looked him directly in the eyes. "John, you are a writer. Tell me how these things came to you."

Grace continued to look in astonishment at the pages of John's notebook as he explained the process, the time periods of work, and how he revised as the song matured. He spoke of the periods of drought corresponding with the times when he was "asleep." John described how now he felt more creative and in tune than ever before, but that something wasn't quite right. As the friends concluded their conversation, Grace encouraged John. "Keep writing. You are a writer."

John was overwhelmed at her support. As he drove away, he wondered, "Would the message come that clearly?"

As the days passed, John thought about the importance of continuing his process of learning music and was determined to see that through. However, he also felt an urgency to meet his purpose with what he could do. "Am I a writer?"

John thought of all the times he said he should write a book, or when a book was written and he would hear people talk about how they should have or could have done it. He felt as though he spent so much time in his own head thinking about life, maybe he should put some of his thoughts down. John didn't have the slightest clue how to do this, but he began to resolve the quest of his gifts by taking one step at a time.

Whether it was lyrics or paragraphs, John found he connected with words. He knew his perspective was different from the mainstream negativity or corporate media. He wondered if people really wanted to hear what he had to say.

John decided that it wasn't his business to worry about other people and their thoughts. "If this is the gift God has given me, then I need to use it." John cleared his throat and prayed, "I believe I have the gift of a different perspective, creativity of thought, and writing. Here I am. Use me to inspire the world."

With all of John's epiphanies, nothing would cause the fear to dissipate. Fear would fight to hold him. He had to be brave. He had to show courage. He had to get vulnerable and stand in front of the world. John's favorite verse from the Bible spoke from his heart, "Be strong and of good courage. For the Lord, your God is with you, wherever you go." John took a step off the cliff of his existence to see if he could live.

CHAPTER NINETEEN
ENGAGE

A funny thing happened on the way to the world's stage. John's perspective was changing. His faith began to deepen as he was seeing the unveiling of his purpose and gifts. Strange occurrences would show themselves in the most auspicious of situations. As John looked for a way to share his perspectives through writing, discussions would manifest with Miguel, Tristan, Denise, and Grace that would serve as signs and a voice for the universe.

It was as if John was traveling in the dark with only a torch to light his path. He was being directed by the light, but only one step at a time. He had a vision for where the journey would lead him, but he couldn't see how to get there. John saw a stadium filled with people coming to hear him speak about the things he would write. He didn't know exactly what he was saying or even the topic, but he saw it.

As John told a friend about this image, the friend responded with, "Imagine the money you will be making!" John wasn't focused on that. He shook off the comment and responded with, "Imagine the lives that I will be able to inspire!" His heart was focused on what mattered—people.

John's response to the friend about money was a bit of a personal shock. He had always worried about having enough, but through this process, he was becoming less concerned with material possessions. His experience made him keenly aware of the tethers that held his life. The variety of debts he had accumulated over the years felt like chains preventing him from being everything he wanted to be. Fear attempted to ambush John from this conversation.

"What if you don't make it? What if you have to leave your job and you can't pay your bills? Your family could be on the street because of you."

Fear is a sly opponent that acts like a boa constrictor on the hunt. It sneaks in through the weeds of practicality, rationality, and responsibility. Then, it strikes your mind with speed. It slides around you with concern and encompasses you with doubt. It squeezes the life out of you with worry and swallows you whole with panic. Fear proves to be the foe within that will try to freeze you from jumping off the cliff.

When it came to fear, John felt he had only two choices: allow it to imprison him where he is, or face it. That's when he came across an acronym that the universe sent: Face Everything And Rise. John knew he was more fearful of living numb and just existing than he was to take a leap into his life's purpose.

He had to engage and stop hiding his gifts. John re-read his first entry in his journal, "Use The Talents God Gave You! Share Them With Others!" So, taking the next step, he started a blog. He titled it: "Awaken and Rise."

John began to post his thoughts, but what was more important was that he was engaging in his gifts. He started the process of growing as a writer and found that he looked forward to blogging every week. He looked forward to posting and the potential impact of the post, believing that someone out there needed to hear the message of hope and love. John was writing to inspire them. He didn't realize it, but he was becoming a more mature version of who he was in high school, before society told him who he had to be. The light showed John another step in the path. It was time to continue forward.

John was contacted by two co-workers who taught a class that focused on preparing high school students for a potential career as a teacher. This class was filled with rich opportunities to interact with younger children and current educators. Through John's blog, the teachers who ran the program, Gillian and Jack, knew they wanted him to come in and share his focus and perspective on education and the power of a teacher.

As John became more vulnerable through his writing, he seemed to draw people in who believed in similar ideas and their discussions were often rich with mutual learning. This was the case with Gillian and Jack. John agreed to share his insights with the class. Though he was unsure that he could give the students the nuts and bolts view of education he thought they wanted, Gillian and Jack assured him that they weren't interested in hearing about that, saying instead, "They need to know the heart of an educator and how this process of education should be approached." After that, John was satisfied that they were on the same page.

Butterflies fluttered through John's body as he stared at the tired but the tolerating audience of 17- and 18-year-olds. He introduced himself and began with his background. The words felt robotic as he discussed the different roles he has fulfilled in his career. It felt too sterile.

John decided to let it go. He cleared his throat, "It was there that I lay face down in the gravel of life. Battered and bloodied with little to show for my impact on the world, I was defeated by the very game that I had mastered. I had no legacy, no memorable history, and no life left within my soul. My body functioned only to exist; my soul was feeling the pressure of inconsequence and regret. Energy escaped me and life was hollow. Why? Because I was more worried about success than I was about my purpose for being in this world."

The class, almost in unison, sat up. Eyes opened wide and students looked at their smiling teachers. "I was once where you are. I wanted to make a difference with my life and help others take their lives to the next level. I decided to be a teacher, a social studies teacher. But what was different for me? I could care less about the content. Don't get me wrong. I worked hard to make sure my students understood the concepts being taught, but that was secondary. I wanted to make a difference in their lives. I wanted to see them find what their heart desired and live their lives fulfilling that desire. I could have been teaching any content. My students were more important and they needed to know that by how I treated each one of them. They weren't just students; they were part of a sacred trust I had been given."

Students were leaning in and intently listening. John continued, "You know the difference. You see it in your education. You know the teacher who is there for you and the teacher who is there to teach the content. Let me say this to you all, if you want to be a teacher because you love a subject, don't. You must love the possibilities that reside in every child you serve. That is first. Period. If you love the content, find a way to use that and find your true purpose in life. Find your gifts. Engage in using them."

John continued to share the concepts he learned. He discussed the importance of spending time in different experiences and asking the tough questions. "Find who you were meant to be and do it! If you think that you can't make a living at it, just remember, someone, somewhere is making a living doing whatever you are hoping to do. Why not you? Don't let society or the world tell you what you can't do. You are more than what a test will ever be able to measure or a system can create." John concluded with conviction and authentic power as he encouraged each student to find the amazing life they were destined to have.

Surprisingly, he kept the attention of the students through the entire 45-minute talk. As students left, a few came up to him and thanked him. They didn't remember hearing a message like this in any of their other classes. Gillian and Jack were grinning from ear to ear. Their appreciation was palpable. The last student to thank John had a question. "What if you love students and you love your content?" she asked.

John was invigorated and he responded simply, "You are in a powerful position to change their lives significantly. Just keep students first."

The student smiled and left with a final comment, "Don't worry. I definitely will."

After spending some closing moments with Gillian and Jack, John went to his car. His hands were shaking. The level of energy within his body was almost more than he could handle. John felt nauseous, excited, incredibly positive, and filled with warmth. He called Tristan. "Tristan, I have to tell you what just happened." John explained the talk and the feeling he felt. He then asked his most important question. "Is this what you feel when you are doing what you love? When you are coaching and teaching? Is this what it is?"

Tristan laughed with utter joy, "Yes! That's exactly it! It's too hard to explain, but you nailed it." After a few more questions, the friends had to end the call and tend to other responsibilities, but John realized he had engaged at a higher level by speaking the words he had been writing. He gained clarity and realized his element. He realized his purpose. It was all clear. John's heart was full and he felt alive. More alive than ever before.

CHAPTER TWENTY
THE POWER DIFFERENTIAL

John sat at home reflecting on the events of the day. He was still energized. John wasn't used to having energy when he got home. Normally, the wear and tear of the day exhausted all he had to give. He usually could force himself to make dinner or engage in some activity, but he never felt like he had anything left to give. John loved his work and his team, but this work wasn't the fuel that drove him. This is the mystery that had eluded John for years as he heard the stories of how people were invigorated by their work. He knew today's opportunity produced energy. John began to think about what he was feeling and how it was impacting him. He searched for other times he felt like this. He thought of the people he knew, or knew of, who lived like this consistently.

John began to realize that every week he would experience a surge of energy when he wrote a blog post. When he finished, he felt more awake than before. John thought of his superintendent who was in constant thought about education, schools, and the work associated with it. He had almost limitless energy to stay in this zone. When John and others needed to take a break, the boss was just getting started.

John thought of the musician who worked diligently through the day and night to write a song only to start again in the morning. He thought of Tristan and how he had the ability to go and push forward with such energy when the team was weary. He remembered how Sir Ken Robinson talked about the synergy associated with people when they are in their element. John realized that finding your gifts and purpose was more than a transaction with the universe, it was a transformation of your life.

He said to himself, "A power differential is in play. When someone is using their gifts in alignment with their purpose, no matter how much time, effort, and energy they put into it, they come out with more life and energy after. It seems as if time almost expands afterwards in honor of adding to the positive purpose of the universe." He grabbed a piece of paper and a pen. John scribbled down this equation.

When you are using your gifts in alignment with your purpose:
$$T+Ef+En < En+T$$

When you aren't using your gifts and not aligned with your purpose:
$$T+Ef+En > En+T$$

    T - is time (conceptual and perceived)
    Ef - is effort (physical work of body)
    En - is energy (spiritual and internal)

"The power differential makes all the difference in the world to the person it is impacting. It is at play all day, every day. It governs our quality of life in many ways and is part of the ripple effect that we have on others," he thought.

John's heart raced as if he were uncovering some ancient secret that was buried within him. He thought of those people who are stuck in a system that governed the quality and regularity of their lives. He thought of those who were miserable working in a job where they were just existing. John believed the power differential is a huge key to their happiness.

He thought, "If you are dragging yourself out of bed in the morning and coming home with no energy, you are in the wrong place in your life. We are incredible beings who weren't meant to be caged by practicality or material needs. We are so much more than that. We have allowed money to govern our lives and our opportunities. We have allowed it to dictate possibilities. We have allowed society to scare us away from our dreams, our gifts, and our purpose."

The words of the Bible echoed in John's mind. "He comes to give you life and give it more abundantly." The abundance of life is found within the power differential. It is the equation that helps a person verify their gifts and purpose. Abundance was becoming real to John. He started to see it as more than just a word, but a condition, an important part of the energy of life.

John decided to test his theory and equation. He knew the first answer, but he needed to start somewhere, so he called Tristan the following day. After the two friends had another discussion of how amazing the experience was for John the day before, John asked the question. "T, I have a thought and need to share it with you. I need you to think of a time when you are doing what you love to do. When you are engaged fully in your gifts and aligned to your purpose."

Tristan laughed and said that he feels he is there most days, but he humored John and put himself in that mindset.

John continued, "When you finish the day and you have given all you have. Are you physically tired?"

"Yeah, to an extent. I mean the body can only run for so long, but I'm not exhausted, if that's what you are asking?" Tristan answered.

"No," John said, "but now I am. Are you exhausted?"

"No, I am not exhausted. I can keep going. It's empowering. Sometimes my body needs a rest and my mind is at peace, but to do the things that really matter, I can keep going."

John noted the response and asked another question, "Let's take this a bit deeper. What about your mind?"

Tristan was deep in thought as silence fell over the phone. "Well, I can tell you that my mind is right. I have control over it and I am at peace. My thoughts focus on the good and the positive. That doesn't mean that I don't have hard times or times of struggle, but it does mean that when I am in the zone, I feel a strong sense of awareness and positive power. I am fulfilled."

John told Tristan why he was asking the questions and the idea of the power differential.

Tristan agreed completely and added, "Not only do I believe this is true, but I can tell you that after I have spent the day in my purpose, the time part is accurate! I feel like I can get it all done and more. I don't know why, but it just seems like my perspective changes and time expands for me." The two spent a few more minutes on the phone before hanging up. When the call ended, John needed to talk to someone who was living the life he used to live. He knew just where to go.

The phone rang and the familiar friendly voice boomed from the other end of the phone, "John, my brother!" Brooks' voice bellowed. "How are you doing?"

"I'm good. You doing well?" John asked.

Brooks immediately switched his tone to an exhausted mix of stress and irritation, "Man, you know how it is. Another day, another person upset, and another irrational situation where adults are foolish or mean-spirited towards each other. The kids are great, they are kids, but the parents are out of control." Brooks had his own school to lead and he was doing it well despite three sets of helicopter parents who wanted to sue each other and the school over athletic playing time and their children being required to follow school rules.

Brooks was worn down by the grind that was leadership, but also by the fact that he wasn't getting the opportunity to use his gifts. He was a gifted people person, mathematician, and actor. He had so much talent, but he was rarely able to use it as he fell into the pressures of needing to lead as a principal. John told Brooks that he wanted to ask him a few questions for some research he was conducting. Brooks willingly answered each question.

"When you finish the day how do you feel?" John started.

"Absolutely destroyed. I go home and just end the night as soon as possible. I get to spend a little time with my family, but I feel like a zombie, just going through the motions," Brooks responded.

"Do you know what your gifts are and the purpose you have in life?"

Brooks took a moment, "Kind of. I know what I enjoy doing and what makes me feel great. I love helping people and taking the time to really get to know them."

John asked, "Do you ever feel like you get to use these gifts?"

Brooks snorted with irritation, "Rarely."

"OK, well when you do get to use them. How do you feel after?"

"Honestly John, I feel like a million bucks. It feels so right and so energizing to do something you are good at and to help people when you are doing it." Brooks' voice had changed with this answer.

John had heard enough. "Brooks, I hope you get to do more of that."

"I need to John. I don't know how much longer I can spend my life in this role. It's changing me," Brooks sounded defeated. John hoped he would rise above the world he was in; someday John hoped to share with him the message of inspiration that was coming together in his heart.

"Anyway, I have a vacation coming soon. Hopefully that will re-energize me and help me get through to the holiday season," Brooks said. "I hope to start the new year refreshed."

John and Brooks talked a little more about the projects they were doing and what they liked about their current jobs. They talked about family and getting together soon. John hoped that it would happen, but he was skeptical due to the nature of Brooks' world and time commitment.

"We'll talk soon," Brooks said.

"Yes, let's talk soon, Brooks." The friends ended the call and John reflected on the conversation. He knew he was on to something. He thought about Brooks relying on vacation to save him. "How long can a vacation energize you if you are miserable in your job and out of alignment with your gifts and purpose?" he wondered. Then John came upon a thought that had been buried deep in his subconscious, but now had his attention. "The goal is to build a life that I don't need a vacation from."

John knew the importance of rest and rejuvenation. He was becoming more aware of the importance of travel and having experiences to open our minds. But he understood that most people use vacation to escape their trapped state. He recognized that most people were trading their year of life for one or two weeks of the year to flee. John was determined to break this cycle in his own life.

It was time for John to jump again. It was time for John to become a professional writer and speaker.

CHAPTER TWENTY-ONE
INTO FOCUS

John began a new stage of his journey and a new level of engagement. He decided to strip everything away from the persona he had built and the image he had portrayed. He was determined to be a more genuine self. John decided that his writing had to go past that of a blog. He needed to chronicle his journey to see life differently. He wanted to give thanks to God and His universe for the lessons he was learning. He wanted to spread the truth that humans are powerful and amazing beings that are greater than the man-made systems and boundaries of possibility created by society. John was fully engaged and determined to inspire the world with his message. He just needed to clear his head.

When it is time to create something new, obstacles most certainly present themselves. As Steven Pressfield discussed in his work, *The War of Art*, the role of resistance is critical, but always present in the creative process. John was not foolish in his journey. He knew it would be filled with hard work, but his blue collar hometown prepared him for such a journey.

John's initial words flowed with intention. He prayed for God to use him. He was broken, unlikely, but available to be used to better the lives of anyone interested. He was ready to burn the ships. He found the first obstacle in his own mind. The thought of how he had wandered for so long kept him tethered to the past and tied to regret.

"Why didn't I realize this sooner? I've wasted so many years. I could've been there for people. I could have been inspiring others to wake up and rise above the lies that the world tells us about our limitations and that the scope of benevolent ambition should not be restricted to what others see as possible."

John would often verbalize this regret to Denise and Grace. They generally held quiet and allowed him to process out of this place of regret. But as the book pushed further into his heart and mind, he regretted more. It began to permeate his thought processes. The old John that had been burned away was attempting to find a way back to life.

John thought it was appropriate to regret and to torture himself with the actions of his past. He thought this was honorable to be disgusted with poor choices and wasted time. He felt as if he were beating up his old self, but he was only serving to resurrect it. John's preoccupation with his past was giving it too much attention and life.

John thought about how he could have been so much more and he didn't need to meander through all the different paths presented to him. If only he would have stayed true to who he was, to the person his parents raised and encouraged. He was angry that he allowed the world and people who didn't really believe in him or know him to plant seeds of doubt. He was angry that his education was a part of destroying his love for books and reading. His anger worked against him. His mind was focused on the scarcity of time and as John developed writer's block, the book came to a halt.

During a weekly lunch, Grace could see something was bothering John. When he told her his thought patterns and how much regret he had for his past, he discussed the anger he had for people who were no longer in his life. Grace calmly said, "But John, don't you think you needed to experience all of it? If for no other reason than to understand what people are going through and to connect with them through your experiences?"

"I guess so, but I would have been so much more. I could have served more," John responded.

"John, you have to remember. You didn't control any of that. What you know now is a direct result of your experience. You can change your future, not your past." Grace spoke the words with urgent kindness.

"Grace, it would have been so much better for everyone had I started years ago." John was then reminded of something he heard before.

Grace responded, "It wasn't time yet John. Whenever I struggle with the past and life situations, I have this card on my dashboard that I keep for such an occasion. It says, 'It's all secretly perfect' and that has carried me through to see a greater reality." There it was again. John previously used this quote to inspire and fuel himself as he went through the awakening process.

At dinner that evening, John told Denise about the conversation he had with Grace. "That's absolutely true," she said. "Look around you." John took a moment and he looked at the walls of his home, initially missing the point.

With a subtle giggle that turned into outright laughter, John's kids, who had not been paying attention to their parents, found themselves being used by God's universe. He immediately diverted his eyes to the little people around the table. His eyes danced. He looked at each one of them. They were all so different, yet so perfect in his eyes.

John then looked into the eyes of his soul mate and saw love and support. She was a better wife and partner than he could have ever imagined being blessed with. Denise and the kids—they were perfect to him. Being here, right now, was perfect. The gifts and purpose he had been given were perfect for him. The message, the journey, the future—it was all secretly perfect.

John's writer's block went away and he feverishly typed during the late evening hours. Denise sat on the couch reading one of John's favorite books and she looked amazing. His heart was full and still growing.

When he finished typing, John sat with his wife and began to visualize the future. Denise saw the wheels turning and asked him what he was thinking about. "I know I am to share this message of hope, love, and purpose. I know that, but I am not sure I know what to share outside of the book. I need something more; something that people can remember. They need something to help them through the process of how to do this; they don't have to wander like I did. Everyone has an acronym and I think I need to find something that works along those lines, but I won't make anything up. I can't fabricate something if it's not genuine. It has to be real," John replied.

"Well, think about your journey. What things meant the most to you? What were the stages? What has God given you to share?" she asked. John was struck with a thought. His book was going to be titled "Awaken and Rise," but what did that really mean?

CHAPTER TWENTY-TWO
RISE

John was certain the idea of "awaken" was self explanatory. "It is the process in which one snaps out of their self-slumber and realizes that there is more to life. It is when a person decides they are ready to journey and discover what their purpose is beyond what the world or society deems is possible. It is the point in which a person stops minimizing God and His universe," he explained to Denise. "But if it is self-explanatory, why did it take me so long? Why was it so hard to see a different life, when I knew my current one was hollow?"

Denise thought for a moment, "Tell me about how you woke up?"

John, mildly frustrated with such an exercise, dug deep into his memory. "It started with a feeling of disconnection and lack of fulfillment. I found work and my daily life to be a complete chore. At first it wasn't so bad, but it became worse over time. I began to forget who I was and why I was doing what I was doing. I saw no purpose in my job and the interactions I cared most about were strained. If I was a ship, I was rudderless and had no star to guide my course."

"But you were doing what you wanted to do, correct?"

"Yes, but it became so disjointed from my dream of inspiring students and developing supportive relationships that I got lost along the way. It wasn't one decision, but several decisions that led me off course. They were all well-intentioned, but wrong responses to the events that took place. Over time, I believed I could achieve through hard work and self-sacrifice alone. It drained me. I became my own martyr. Everything was a fight and people weren't seen as people. I saw them as allies or enemies. I forgot about kindness, love, and purpose. If you weren't for me, you were against me. It was a fight. I guess when you're too busy fighting, you spend very little time loving. I didn't know why, but I lost myself. In the end, the adulation, recognition, and awards that I sought to validate all of this weren't enough to fill the gaps left by abandoning my purpose."

"OK. So how did you wake up?" Denise was more determined to help John. She knew he was circling the answer, but he needed to realize it. He needed to say it.

"I was miserable and I knew it. I spent time thinking about why I felt the way I did. I blamed everyone. I blamed situations, people, and institutions, but I didn't stop there. I believed I was the victim and I don't play the victim very well. I know that I am powerful. I know that I am here to make a difference. I know that others have made a difference before me and when I thought about their lives, the realization that they refused to be a victim echoed strongly."

"John, you are getting close." Pausing between each word she asked, "What made you wake up?"

"Once I stopped blaming situations, people, and institutions,

I began to see myself as an equal- no, a more powerful player in creating my destiny. I decided to look for the good, the positive, and the inspirational. I decided I would no longer live as a victim who was traveling a path dictated to me, but that I would choose to find my higher life. I couldn't live life asleep any longer. I wanted fulfillment, connection, and meaning. I prayed for these things and I intentionally asked God to show me how to get there."

"And there it is!" Denise laughed.

John sat stunned realizing that his sleep was partly put upon him, but it was also self-inflicted due to his growing negative and powerless view of himself. He couldn't see it because of his lack of willingness to spend time in reflection. Instead, he preferred to blame the previous reasons. When John woke up, it didn't happen overnight; but it did happen because he asked for it. He wanted it. He needed it. John was willing to give himself to the concept of "awaken." He put away pride and opened his heart and mind to new learning. God loves it when we are willing. Sometimes He is just waiting for us to say so.

"Now rise?" John paused for a few minutes in thought. "Rise. Oh, I know what rise is," he stated confidently in the moment of epiphany.

"Don't just sit there talking to yourself. What is it?" Denise asked.

"R - Recalibrate. I had to recalibrate who I was and what was truly important. I had to shut out the world and decide that I would determine what I valued. The days of defining myself by what others thought and restricting my options to their boundaries were over. It was a process of recapturing who I was and centering myself on a greater life.

"I - Inspire yourself and others. Invest in your energy and spend time meeting the needs of others. It is a period of gaining internal fuel for the journey. All the words, books, videos, and conversations were providing me energy for the hard work needed in the next two stages. As I was inspired by others, I found myself believing in the possibilities of recreating myself and my future.

"S - Seek your gifts and purpose. I've heard some people talk about a specific path of finding one or the other, but I believe it comes to you as it is supposed to, and it is all secretly perfect. We are all powerful in our gifts and purpose. We cannot allow anything to get in the way of finding where we belong and how we fit into the universe. God has a journey for all of us that's often interrupted by doubt, lack of purpose, and perceived restriction of possibilities. With all that being said, our gifts and purpose help us get to a higher level. They take us to the edge of the cliff of existence so that we can jump and soar with life. Our gifts and purpose are more than what the Steve Harvey video suggested. Its results are more than travel and material possessions; the results are a path to fulfillment and joy. It's a way for us to connect to the universe and make a difference for everyone. Finding your gifts and purpose is a critical step to fulfillment and joy.

"E - Engage is the most critical step. It isn't enough to just do the other three steps, I had to complete it. I had to engage in my gifts and purpose. I had to see what life was like when I wrote and shared my heart. I had to feel the energy of speaking to that class to know I was on the right path. I gave my energy to the universe and it came back in droves which led me to the concept of the Power Differential.

That is R.I.S.E." John was energized as he finished. Denise was smiling. She was proud of her husband.

"That is awesome and true!," she said. "Now, don't sit on it. Share it with someone. Then someone else. Then someone else, until you've shared it with the world."

CHAPTER TWENTY-THREE
WE MEET AGAIN

John's knowledge of how to write a book was non-existent. All he knew was that he had to share his story of hope. Once he realized what he had gone through, he wanted to help those who were experiencing disillusionment and disconnection. He wanted to be used to inspire people to find their higher life. John tried to write at home, but with three little ones running about and a neighborhood filled with kids who loved to come over and play, he struggled. John tried early morning sessions. He tried night sessions. Nothing seemed to work.

One evening, Denise was taking the kids on a few errands and John was beginning to write.

"Instead of writing here and getting in the groove only to have us potentially interrupt it when we get back, why don't you go to the coffee shop down the road?" she suggested.

"That's a good idea." John repacked the laptop and headed out the door. He entered the coffee shop with a bit of timidity. Kefi Coffee was the name of this place and he had no idea what it meant. As he cracked open the glass door, his eyes feasted on the colors, the decor, and the smiles upon the face of the patrons. This place had a different vibe and a more welcoming spirit than many of the library-like atmospheres of some coffee institutions. It was warm, artistic, and had a sense of connectedness to people. John knew immediately that he loved this place.

John ordered a latte and set up shop at a comfortable chair and table. He started to write slowly and methodically about his journey. He emptied his heart and soul onto the illuminated electronic pages that had been waiting for his words. When he finished the first draft of the introduction, John began to outline the chapters in a disjointed fashion. He tried to bring some semblance of order to what would follow.

As he finished this simple outline that would structure the story, John heard a familiar voice. He looked up to see the back of a recognizable head. John's heart filled with a great desire to become invisible. He kept his head down and stayed focused on being quiet. However, he saw in his peripheral that the person had turned and recognized him.

John thought for certain he would have to partake in some form of trite false pleasantry, but the other person seemed like he wanted to be invisible too. John became curious and felt his heart open. He looked up from his writing.

"Hello Mack."

"Hello John."

Mack's nervousness became palpable. He began tapping his fingers and shifting back and forth waiting for his coffee. The book in Mack's hand suggested that he wasn't taking this to go.

John could tell that Mack was scanning for a place to sit. The only open spot was next to John. Mack was one of the negative crew from John's old school, Hyde Park, and his hatred of John was awakened at the sight of his former boss. Mack paid for his coffee and the owner of the shop asked Mack if the two men knew each other. Mack explained that they used to work in the same place and you could tell that he was internally praying for the owner to not ask any follow-up questions about their former interactions. The answer to his prayer was "no."

"Oh that's great! Did you two plan to meet tonight? He must have saved a seat for you," the owner said with a smile.

Mack laughed nervously, "No, just a coincidence."

"A sign," John thought.

Mack scanned to see if anyone was getting up from their tables and no one seemed to be leaving. John looked kindly at Mack and said, "Hey Mack, don't mind me. I'm focused on writing. I won't distract you from your book."

Mack tried to be pleasant, but his disdain for John still lingered in his heart. "Thanks, John." Mack sat down and John saw the book that he was about to read: *The Alchemist*.

Mack wanted to stay within his own head. He didn't want to talk to John, but his nervousness and irritation that John was next to him overpowered his want of solitude into an eruption of small talk. John should have been just as agitated at Mack's intrusion into his writing time, but it seemed meant to be.

Finally, Mack let it slip, one simple phrase that moved the conversation from small talk to substance. As Mack was asking about

John's current role, he said, "I'm sure things are better without having me around you."

"Why would you say that?" John's coyness was further irritating Mack.

"Come on, John. You don't like me and I certainly don't like you. We can stop pretending. I've spent the last several years despising you and your unfair treatment of me. You don't have to act like you care now. We can just move on and..."

"I know, Mack, but what if I told you I felt the same way?"

Mack surprised said, "What did I ever do to you? You were the one who came in and drew a line in the sand with all of us. You're the one who made me and others feel like we weren't valued. You are the one who made me hate my job. In fact, I could barely get up in the mornings when I worked with you. You made me miserable and I still am. You have ruined me as a teacher."

He absorbed the tense but quiet tirade from Mack. Mack's frustration was growing as he believed John's lack of reaction was a sign of not caring.

"One last thing and I'll stop. In the future, I hope you remember that the people you have to work with can be your greatest assets, if you don't ruin them."

"Well since we are blunt with each other, I can't say that I was perfect Mack. Frankly, I was far from it. But did you know that you were miserable before I got to Hyde Park?"

"No, that's not true."

"It sure is. I didn't know you before, but your colleagues did. They told me about you. If you remember, I walked in the door and welcomed you. I trusted you, until I found out about how you were talking behind my back and trying to shut down the changes we needed to put in place. You say I didn't care about you, but the truth is, Mack, you lost your love for kids, if you ever had it. You became concerned with yourself and what made you comfortable.

"Yet, you weren't the only one to make mistakes. I made them too. I saw people as friends or enemies. I did draw a line in the sand. I was selfish in the quest to build a legacy to communicate the importance of my life. I wanted to do something great to make my time count. What mattered was the result and not the people I was given the opportunity to serve. You share this selfishness, except you were focused on keeping things your way. You didn't want to push yourself to grow and get uncomfortable. You wanted to believe you were great just as you were." Mack sat stunned and John continued.

"You were uncaring towards students, unless they fit the mold of what you deemed acceptable. You were cold and unconcerned about their needs. Yes, I saw you as an enemy and I didn't get through to you. However, the reality I wanted to show you was you can't make a difference for kids or those around you by refusing to grow. I was hoping to inspire you to be the teacher I thought you could be, but you refused. So you became an enemy to my mission."

When John finished a hush fell over the men. Mack was angrily processing what John said. He didn't like what he had heard, but something inside of him caused him to continue to pause and reflect. Mack was puzzled by John's admittance of his own faults. He wanted to hate John, but for some reason he was curious to why John would put that in the discussion.

"Fine. I don't agree with you, but did you know you were making mistakes at the time?"

"Of course not! I thought I was right. The world was black and white. I was driven by a mission to make my time there count and to achieve at the highest levels of our profession. Unfortunately, I lost myself long before I got to Hyde Park. But during my time there, I fell deeper into a sleep that caused me to simply exist. I was unhappy, unfulfilled, disconnected, and asleep to the truth. It took me a long time to realize this problem, but I am thankful that I am a much different person now than before. Not perfect, just different."

Silence fell again on the two men. John was nervous that he went too deep and he thought Mack would check out of the conversation. His former colleague stayed silent as he looked at the cover of his book. John reminded himself this wasn't a coincidence.

"What do you mean that you were asleep and unfulfilled?"

"To give you the shortest version possible, I struggled with who I was growing up. I struggled with figuring out what I should do with my life. Education provided me an avenue to inspire students, especially those who were on the fringes of the school experience. I wanted to inspire them to chase their dreams and live an uncommon life. But along the way, I got distracted by my ego and its desire to gain accolades, awards, and achievements. My sleep was the utter hold these desires had on me. I began to believe that my life could only matter if people told me that I was great and achieved great things in their eyes. I lost my purpose. I was failing while gaining all the success the world had to offer. Even though I felt miserable and drifted from the person I was meant to be, I doubled down on these lies. I almost refused to see meaning and success in their truest forms and simply looked for the adulation and recognition of achievement. In the end, I felt hollow and disconnected. I lived life in a state of existence.

"When I finally realized this, I had a choice to make. I could stay asleep and continue to feel miserable and exist from moment to moment; or I could awaken and rise to a life worth living. A life that offered fulfillment and connection. A life of purpose beyond myself. A life where I could soar."

Mack again sat silent. John took a sip of his drink and Mack swirled the remains of his cup before taking one last gulp. It was as if John could see Mack's mind working as he stared at the artwork on the walls of the coffee shop.

"What does Kefi mean?" Mack asked as the owner walked past.

"It's a Greek word that's difficult to define, as it is more of a feeling, but it means joy, passion, and exuberance."

"Interesting." Mack whispered.

"John, I'm not going to sit here and tell you that I am over what happened at Hyde Park, but you have me curious. I have to leave, but would you be willing to meet again and talk more? I would like to hear more about how you woke up."

"I'm fine with that and I would love to tell you that I am over everything as well, but I'm not. However, I am working on it."

"How is Saturday around 2:00 PM?"

"See you then, Mack."

John rushed home to find Denise having a rare moment of peace as the kids were playing in their rooms. He was excited to share his encounter and the conversation that followed. Denise was intently listening to John as he recapped his evening.

"Looks like you've found the first person to share your message with."

CHAPTER TWENTY-FOUR
THE KING OF PAIN

John arrived at the coffee shop early on Saturday since he desperately wanted to get some writing finished before Mack arrived. He settled into a larger table to set up and get to work, but once he was ready to begin, the door opened and Mack walked in. Mack had *The Alchemist* in hand and he nodded when he saw John.

"I was coming in early to get some reading done, but it looks like you had the same idea."

"I guess it was meant to be, Mack."

Mack bought a tea as the owner of the shop remarked how we are here together twice in one week.

"Where you get one, you get the other," he laughed.

"At least we planned this one, well, sort of planned," John laughed.

Mack sat down and put his book on the table. He tried to act casual, but something was stirring inside of him. No pretend small talk was needed today. Mack jumped in.

"John, I don't want to waste your time and definitely not mine.

I've spent a lot of time thinking about what you said the other night and I want to know one thing. Are you being honest with me? Is this some kind of game to rebuild your image or something?"

John looked directly into Mack's soul.

"This is absolutely the truth. I haven't been more serious about anything like this in a long time. As far as my image goes, I'm done with worrying about how the world sees me. Do I want to connect with people and heal the wounds from our past? Yes, I do. However, it isn't about what I can gain, but what I can give."

"Thanks for answering that."

"Alright," John said with a warm smile.

"But before we dig in," Mack stammered. "I am going to say this. You were correct on one thing. I was miserable before you came to Hyde Park. You made me more miserable and I am still not ready to move past it, but I want to acknowledge that it wasn't all you. You just intensified it."

"Fair enough, Mack. I think at this point before I go further into what happened with me, I need to ask something of you."

"Are you kidding? I knew there would be a catch to this! What do you want from me a letter of recommendation? You want me to tell people you weren't the colossal jerk that you were?"

John had to take a deep breath. He could feel the heat rising in his body as he was fighting back the urge to verbally take Mack on. John paused for a moment longer and thought of his purpose. He reflected on what he wanted to share with Mack. John took a drink to collect his thoughts and swallow his anger.

"No, Mack. That's not me anymore. I am asking from this

point on to give me your word that our discussion stays completely and simply honest. No agendas, you don't need to tell people we have shared a coffee or even the same space, but let's be honest with each other."

Mack was surprised at the request and embarrassed by his response. "I can do that."

"Great. When we spoke the other night, I shared with you how I was asleep and feeling hollow. What made you want to hear more?"

"Curiosity and I want to hear more about how miserable you were." Mack chuckled. "And... I am in a tough space myself. I mean, my life. I guess my life isn't what I thought it would be and..." Mack trailed off for a moment. "And...I'm not happy. I'm struggling and I have been struggling for years. Before you came to Hyde Park, I spent several years in teaching and I lost my way, I became, as you shared, disconnected and started feeling hollow. As you told how you were sleeping your words were communicating the pain I feel, but your face was leading me to believe that you aren't in that place anymore."

"You are correct. I am not in that place anymore."

"How did it change for you? How did you get the happiness and the hope to return to your life?"

"That's a great question and I'm going to answer it, completely."

John spent the next hour telling Mack all the twists and turn of his story. He shared the car wreck, the realizations he had while in the hospital, how focusing on powerful words helped to change his behaviors and perspectives. John told Mack of his failings as a husband and father. He told the story of the email he received from Reuben, and his struggle to awaken from his sleep. He discussed the concept and the power of R.I.S.E. and where he sees his life going due to his discovery of the power differential. John shared it all.

Mack was fascinated, and during the course of John's vulnerable story of his failings and the truth that he found on the other side of those failures, he began to see John as a human being. Mack began to feel a connection. When John finished his nearly uninterrupted hour of sharing, Mack sat back in his chair.

"Wow, John. I can't believe how much I hated you all this time, thinking that you were such a know-it-all and a royal jerk. You were struggling to figure it all out just like the rest of us. I'm sorry for how much I hated you and for how I still disliked you coming in here today. Can you forgive me?"

John was shocked at the request. He never believed he would hear those words. "I do, Mack. Can you forgive me?"

"Yes, I forgive you."

"Thank you Mack. Now I'm ready to move past with you."

"Same here. Well, since we are friends now or at least not enemies," Mack said with a sarcastic smile, "Would you help me with what you went through? Would you help me wake up and rise up? Is that how you say it?"

John smiled, "Awaken and rise, and there is nothing I would rather do than to help you. A few things you must understand. This isn't easy work. This is difficult, time-intensive, reflection-intensive, and vulnerable work. However, it is worth every minute. In the end, you will find a greater sense of purpose and peace with who you are and how you can make an impact on the world. By changing you, you are changing the world."

Mack sighed, "Can we just start with me first. That's a lot of pressure."

"That's the whole point. There is no pressure to change the world. Just by taking the step to make a change for yourself and in yourself, you will make a difference to the world. All you have to worry about is you. The rest will fall into place. No pressure at all. You just have to be you."

"I'm ready. What do I need to do? Don't tell me I need to have an accident or something cataclysmic to change my view. What can I do that is tangible? What is something simple?"

"Mack there isn't anything simple about what takes place, but the questions I have for you will be simple."

John asked Mack four questions:

1. Why do you want to wake up?

2. How do you see yourself?

3. What are you looking to gain?

4. Are you truly willing to give yourself over to the process no matter how hard and how difficult it is to complete?

"Don't answer these now. Let's meet here Monday evening at six o'clock. Take your time and think about them. Write ideas and thoughts down as you process this and allow your heart to speak as loud as your head."

Mack agreed to a meeting on Monday and he thanked John for sharing his life's story. John was excited to be able to share his heart with Mack while Mack was excited that his life had the option to change for the better.

CHAPTER TWENTY-FIVE

MONDAYS WITH MACK

Mack was waiting on John in a quiet corner of the coffee shop reading his book. On the side table, he had a journal with a pen. Mack had spent the last two days in thought as he struggled to find the right answers to John's questions. He wrote his ideas, thoughts, answers, and sometimes drew pictures to represent what he was thinking.

He was eagerly anticipating John's arrival. The time seemed to be crawling. When he realized that it was slightly past six o'clock, he sat up and strained his neck to see if he could gaze into the parking lot. Mack was muttering irritable thoughts as John opened the door. He instantly calmed his negativity and waved to John.

"I'm sure glad to see you," John's voice boomed. "I wondered after our last meeting if I might have scared you off."

"John, I'm not going to say this isn't scary so far, but the idea that my life can regain its hope and purpose is stronger than any fear I may be dealing with. That's why I committed to this process."

"So what did you think of those questions I gave you?"

"They were extremely difficult and I can't say that I have them completely answered, but here's what I have so far." Mack took a moment to open his journal and clear his throat. "Why do I want to wake up?" he said sheepishly. "I am tired. I'm tired of feeling like I'm always fighting against everything. No matter how safe I play it, my life is filled with battles and for some reason people who want to make things miserable for me tend to gravitate my way. I want to see life differently. I want what you have. The brightness in the eyes, the belief in self, the mentality that you are living above the drama and the fray. I want to feel alive without being dragged through the mud of constant drama and misery."

John looked off in thought and Mack waited for feedback.

"Next question, how do you see yourself?" John queried.

"This was exceptionally difficult. I'm a father, a husband, teacher, and I may be sarcastic, but I do genuinely care. I am impatient. I get angry easily. I don't take direction well. I attract drama. I enjoy music and occasionally like to read. I guess I'm a decent guy who has flaws, but wants to be better."

"Question number three, what are you looking to gain?"

Mack was somewhat bothered by the lack of feedback from John. He began to feel as though he was wasting his time.

"OK, I think I said this before, but I am looking to gain a better life. I want to feel alive without having to get beat up over and over again without anything changing. I want to end my misery, gain connection and fulfillment."

"Are you truly willing to give yourself over to the process no matter how hard and how difficult it is to complete?

"Yes, that's why I'm here. That's why I'm answering these

questions. That's why I have spent time trying to figure this out." Mack paused with doubt about what he was going to let leave his lips, but he succumbed to his impulse.

"John, do you know what you are doing? I'm not trying to be disrespectful, but I haven't heard any response. Do you know what to say? Is this a waste of time?"

"Mack these aren't right or wrong answers, but more of a chance for you to figure yourself out. I can't dictate any of these answers to you, but I will tell you some of them will change. Question number one, your reasons are yours and yours alone. They better come from the heart and be enough to sustain you when things get difficult and frustrating. Only you know if they are, but I will remind you of these when things get tough. Question two should change dramatically over time, but I want to return to this later. Question three, again this is your answer alone. It connects to question number one, but it focuses you on your future. Question one is about the past, question three is about your future. Question two, it's a 'how do you see yourself' realization. Question four is straightforward. You are verbalizing your commitment. No conditions, no exceptions, it is an opportunity to send out into the universe where you stand. When you struggle, revisit this question and recite your answer to yourself and to the universe."

"Sorry John. This is new to me and I wanted to give you the benefit of the doubt, but I needed more. I'm glad I asked."

"The only question I want to address is number two. Is that all you are?"

Mack was stunned by John's return question.

"All? That's a lot, John."

"Mack, you spent more time on your faults, the roles you fulfill, and who you currently are. What I want to challenge you on is, who are you really? At your core, at the being that is Mack, is that all there is?"

"I hope I don't burst your bubble, but I'm not a spiritual kind of guy. I feel as though I am limited here."

"I understand you, but Mack are you a copy?"

"A copy?"

"Yes, a copy. When you were born, did the pages of history copy and paste a person from years ago and produce you?"

"Mack laughed at the reference. I suppose not and I get what you are saying."

"I'm not sure you do. Let me say this. There is no one else like you. You are one of a kind. One in billions upon billions of people who have walked the face of the earth. No one else has ever been here who is just like you. No one who has your strengths, flaws, and abilities. No one in history. Period. You are a uniquely created being with power beyond measure to grow and impact those around you. You don't need to be spiritual to see that fact. You are here in this time with all of your abilities and flaws to relate and create a wonderful ripple effect for those who you are in your world. That is who you are and you will only grow more impactful over time as you embrace this reflection of your true self."

"Maybe you're right," Mack said with a bit of hesitation. "It's just...it's just this life can be so hard at times. Trying to live up to expectations, to know who has an opinion you should care about, and to establish some form of comfort, it's completely exhausting. I feel like I spend too much time being someone I'm not."

"Who are you?" Before Mack could respond, John finished, "That is the essential purpose of what we are doing here. Getting to the core of who you are and finding the connection and joy that you deserve. We are searching for your purpose. It's only in and through your purpose that you can experience all the things that you want to get out of this process. Let me ask you another question. Why are you a teacher?"

Mack paused for a long period of time. He thought back to the early days of his college career when he was going to be a chemist. He remembered how bored he became doing lab work and the endless calculations that followed. He drifted further back in time to his middle school days where he was inspired by a teacher who loved sharing the wonders of science with his students. Mack remembered tutoring friends in high school and the energy he would find when he helped his lab partners in college. He remembered the day when he realized teaching was at the heart of who he was. He immediately changed his major and chased the dream with vigor.

"I guess I really enjoyed helping people unlock the mysteries of science and the look on their faces when they understood something they didn't realize until that moment. I enjoyed the connection and struggle to help someone discover knowledge."

"How do you feel about it now?"

"I'm miserable. The parents, the kids who don't care, the government interference, these tests that measure nothing important, and the constant flow of negative perceptions of educators makes me hate every moment of it."

"Why do you stay in it then?"

"What else am I to do? I used to love it, but now, I don't know what else I can do with my life," Mack was sullen in his response. "I'm stuck."

"Stuck is a perception and it's rooted in fear. We can't think clearly when we are encompassed by fear. Remember who you are Mack. You are powerful. I need to help you access that power."

Mack wouldn't look John in the eyes. He was sinking deeper within himself.

"Mack, why do you want to wake up? Are you willing to give yourself over to this process?"

"I want connection and a life of joy. I am."

"Mack, you are waking up. It's never easy to get out of a deep slumber, but you are doing it. Embrace the power you have and think about how unique of a person you truly are. You are the only *you* in history. If you believe that, all of these things that are dragging you into drama and through the mud of life, they no longer have power over you. Let's take one thing. Just one and demonstrate your power this week. What is the most negative thing you have experienced recently?"

"I am really struggling with the negativity from our current principal. It seems as if he wants to make things so difficult, but not like you did. He consistently makes negative comments to me and my co-workers. Then everyone comes to me with these issues so it feels like I'm dealing with all of it."

"This is a great situation. Instead of struggling with your potential answers and letting the negativity compound on top of you, why don't you find a way to see this as an opportunity to spread kindness? Do this and let's come back together next Monday to talk about what you see. Be observant. Don't just focus on your action, but look at the results of your action."

CHAPTER TWENTY-SIX

THE RESULTS ARE IN

Monday came and John settled in at the coffee shop. Mack popped through the door in unusual fashion. He made a straight line for John. Something big was on the tip of his tongue; he sat down, brimming with vitality.

"Did you know this would happen?"

"What happened? What do you mean?"

"Everything happened! It was an unbelievable week! When we left, I spent time thinking about how I could spread kindness in my world. I decided to start by complimenting my fellow teachers. I wanted them to know how much they mattered to our kids, parents, and staff. The looks on their faces were priceless. A few were stunned and looked at me as if I was losing my mind. I could tell it was the last thing they imagined coming from my mouth. Then on Wednesday, I wrote thank you notes to our guidance counselors for how they support our students and families," Mack was beaming with excitement.

"Thursday was a test of my patience. I ran into our principal and he made one of his notoriously rude comments about me trying to build influence in the staff by being nice. I took a breath and thanked him for being our principal. I told him I am realizing leadership positions are lonely and stress-filled. I finished with, 'thank you for doing a thankless job.' On Friday, I felt so good about what I was doing with staff, I wanted to share it with students. I thanked them when they were kind to each other, when they worked hard, and when they came to me for help. Today, my class started like never before, my students worked harder, they were kinder, and they started helping each other. Then to top it all off, I heard about how someone had written a thank you note to another colleague. Kindness and gratitude were spreading. None of the players had changed, but something was changing in them!"

"Do you remember question number two?" John queried.

"The how do I see me question?"

"That's the one. How do you see yourself?"

Mack could now see it. "I am powerful. I am kind. I have the ability to make a difference."

"Exactly! Remember how this all started. How miserable you were and how you blamed everyone around you for how you felt?" John asked.

"I do remember."

"Well, regardless of what is happening around you, know that you are the powerful one. The only power others have over you is the power you give to them. This is the first step. Awaken to who you are and the power you have within you by simply being your best self. No complaining, no destructive self-comments, and no giving your power away to others. When you had a focus for kindness, it grew to gratitude.

When you're grateful, you cannot help but to be aware of the good that is within you and the good that surrounds us. It's all about perspective. Sometimes it's not easy, but it is true all the time."

"Come on John, not all the time."

"Yes, all the time. Even in personal tragedy there is so much good happening, but we have to put away the lens of hate, hurt, and fear to see it. Let me tell you a quick instance where this is evident. Years ago when I was starting out, I had to push a teacher who wasn't doing her job into retirement. She was once a fantastic teacher, but over the years she became bitter and negative. Her performance was poor at best, and her relationships with students were non-existent. She hated me, but I had to do my job and students were in need of someone to stand for them. After the retirement paperwork was completed, she continued to drag my name through the mud. Every so often, I would hear another story of how she was attempting to trash my reputation, but suddenly I heard nothing. It was as if she was gone. Years later, I received a letter from her. It started with how much she despised me and how she spent a few years after being forced to leave teaching doing everything in her power to destroy the reputation I was building."

"So how is this supposed to inspire me John? Sounds pretty bleak. She sounds bitter."

"The second part of the letter shared the story of how her husband became very sick and needed her. She started to realize that if she was teaching, she wouldn't have been able to be there for them. She told me about the two years she spent being by his side and holding his hand as he passed. She thanked me for doing such a difficult job and for helping her into a phase of her life that she refused to accept.

She knew that if she was teaching, she would have missed all that time. Instead of losing a career, she gained the precious final moments with her husband."

"Wow!" Mack exclaimed. "At first she was a lot like where I was, but I see what you're saying. If she would've been focused on what she didn't have instead of what she was actually being given, she would still be that same bitter person. Her gratitude towards that unexpected and unwanted gift of retirement meant more to her in the end."

"Exactly Mack. She was being given something more important. Had she failed to realize this and change her perspective, she would still be unhappy. Once she decided to see the good, she stopped destroying herself with that bitterness and she began to empower herself with gratitude. It's all in how you choose to see it."

"I get it, but now what?"

"I'm certain you are awake, Mack. I know it."

"And now?"

"Now, you RISE."

"Rise?"

"Recalibrate, Inspire, Seek, and Engage. Once I was awake, this is the process that I went through to find purpose and joy."

Mack paused, then asked, "Once I do this, I'll find connection and joy?"

"Yes, but it isn't a one-time thing. It's a formula to overcome disillusionment. It keeps us grounded in our purpose. It's something that I do daily. Within RISE, you find purpose and meaning."

"OK. How do I recalibrate?" Mack was on the edge of his seat. His zeal for the process was visible and his heart was ready to take on the challenge.

"We do this by asking ourselves the right questions. Who am I? What is important to me? What really matters? What is the big picture?"

"Wait, I already answered who I am."

"You did. That question is the bridge from understanding the power you have by being uniquely you to searching your soul and figuring out your bearings. Recalibrate yourself through the power of reflection and strip away all the distraction of what the world tells you to value. What do you truly value? This is something most people don't spend the time to discover. It is hard reflective work. It often leads us to default to what the society tells us to value. It's easier, but in the end, it hurts who we are."

The two men talked at length about these questions. John simply provided questions that allowed Mack to dive deeper into what mattered in his core. Mack was uncovering truths about himself that he had long forgotten. He was feverishly writing in his journal as they discussed ideas and answers. Finally, they realized the time and they were both late in getting home. Mack stood up with John and he extended his hand. John shook it and he could feel the gratitude from Mack. Mack, held back by history, found it hard to say thanks after all he had been through. Even with forgiving John at their earlier meeting, he held back. Mack felt too much emotion. He sensed a lack of control over it and simply nodded to John. John smiled and said, "Until we meet next week. Keep doing the things you're doing at work. Be the source of kindness and gratitude as you decide on the answers to the questions."

CHAPTER TWENTY-SEVEN
NOT MUTUALLY EXCLUSIVE

Mack and John settled into their routine as both were thrilled with the results of their meetings. When they began their discussion of Mack's recalibration, he was ready. He spent the week reconnecting with his wife, co-workers, and friends. Mack wanted to get to the root of what people perceived mattered most to him. He analyzed their perceptions. He was able to make specific determinations about what made an impact on him and where he became distracted from being the real Mack. Armed with information and reflective thought, Mack waited for the question.

"Glad you had a productive week, Mack. I had a great week myself. What do you think about the questions from last week?"

Mack described the process of the last week. He told John about all the information he used to guide his reflection. He told John how much he appreciated the questions and then shared his answers.

"What's important to me? What matters to me? What matters in the big picture? John, these aren't mutually exclusive questions. In fact, they are very much connected. My family, my friends, and my students are all important to me. But what matters most in my big picture is the impact I can have on them. I value my opportunity to touch their lives through what I do.

"What matters is the energy I put into their worlds. And yes John, teaching matters a great deal to me. I thrive off of the idea of a student understanding concepts and unlocking knowledge. The moment when they gain that empowerment and know they have accomplished what was once impossible in their minds. That's what matters to me, but I want to add something new. My faith. When this process started, I didn't know what mattered and I didn't know if God or His universe cared much for me. However, after seeing the impact I have had in two weeks with kids, colleagues, and my own family, I know that I am here for a reason."

John's smile grew wide and his heart warmed, "Now that you see the truth, start looking for what He is saying to you. God is always talking to us, it's just a matter of whether or not we are willing to look and listen."

John had a moment of déjà vu as he heard Grace's words leave his mouth in helping Mack. It was becoming clearer to John that not only was he in his purpose, but that Grace was placed in his life to serve as his guide along this road. It helped him realize that he wasn't haphazardly guiding Mack, but that he was being used by God, through an interconnected network of people, to make the world better. John began to think, "People are so important to God that He moves heaven and earth to reach them one person at a time. We only need to be willing and available to be a part of this magnificent process."

"Let's summarize it, Mack. What matters to you? What's your unchangeable core?"

"Family, friends, faith, empowering, and supporting others", Mack proudly stated.

"Next, we need to spend time surrounding you with things that will keep you focused and inspired. Know that resistance will push back and you have to be fueled to push through it. Words and images matter. Fill your self with strong words and images that keep you dialed in to what matters most. This is critical," John emphasized.

The two men spent the next hour on John's laptop finding videos, quotes, and anything else that would help Mack remind himself of his focus. Mack was particularly drawn to a poster he wanted for his classroom. It was titled "You Are" and it had statements below the title stating, "You are scientists, you are explorers," but at the bottom in big bold lettering, it said, "You Are The Reason I Am A Teacher". Mack felt it centered his focus. It was a daily visual to recalibrate and fuel himself with inspiration.

John looked at Mack and he could see a difference. There was a different energy about him. John remembered the torturous time he had in getting to where Mack was in this process, but Mack wasn't struggling the way he once did. This made John realize that the process is different for every person who takes this journey. He felt honored to share this message and knew it was time for the next step.

"Mack, we have the first half in place. You're awake. You know how to recalibrate, you have your inspiration, now you need to seek your gifts and purpose. I think you're really close."

Mack sat quietly waiting for John's next words.

"Another question for you. If you had one year to live and the only way to extend your life was to do the one thing that your heart desired above all else, what would it be?"

"This would have been a hard question for me when we first started this. I thought for certain my days as an educator were numbered. But now that I've looked past all the distractions, I know I'm doing exactly what my heart desires most: teaching. I'm a bit unsure of what my gifts are, but my purpose is to empower and support students in their learning. This is all encompassing. When I say all, I don't mean the ideal students, but all of them. Yes, the ones that you used to push me to try and connect with, but I stubbornly resisted out of pride, anger, and fear."

"I'm curious about that last word, fear. Please tell me more."

"I was afraid that I couldn't cut it. I didn't know how to find a way to connect. It was so difficult to gain their interest and trust that it was easier to give up and be angry. It was easier to manage their lack of interest by ignoring them. I told myself for years that they were failing. The reality is that I was failing because I was frozen in fear. If I tried and failed, it meant I couldn't do it. It was a knock on me. But if I could make it their issue, then it was their failure. Not mine.

"Here's the kicker, I am still afraid of failing them, but I'm more afraid of being who I was: bitter and angry, no zeal for life. It's worth it to step out and try. It's like that video you asked me to watch. If I want to fly in life, I have to jump. And I do want to fly. Because if I can fly, it means that my students are going to fly. That is my ripple effect."

John was astounded at how much Mack had absorbed. He

was almost speechless. "I didn't realize how much you've been taking in, my friend. What you just said is fantastic. You know what your purpose is, but what are your gifts? Think of your gifts as the vehicle you use to get to the starting point of purpose. What is going to enable you to empower and support all students?"

The two bantered back and forth with the usual process of John asking questions and Mack pausing for reflection then answering. Then John would follow up with more questions based on Mack's answer. It took awhile and both men had to call home to let their wives know they were going to be home later than expected.

With Kefi Coffee set to close in less than an hour, Mack was getting tired, but John was fueled to continue on. It was the Power Differential in play for John, but Mack was at his limit. He wasn't weary of the topic, but it had been a long day. Finally, John asked Mack, "When you used to help classmates, tutor lab partners, and you realized you wanted to be a teacher, what did you use to be successful?"

"I listened to them, I found a way to relate the learning to their lives. I would connect what they already knew to where they needed to go. I would then break it down step by step. My focus was on pushing them to struggle through the tough parts by finding their own parallels to the learning."

John sat back and folded his arms. "My friend, you just revealed your gifts."

"What I just said? Those are gifts?" Mack asked with a puzzled look on his face.

"Yes. All too often we see gifts as being a tangible or measurable quality, and maybe ultimately they are, but we don't have the sophistication to measure what you have described. You have the gift to connect with people, to draw out their interests, and help them apply it to new concepts. You have the gift to show them how to unlock their own ability to understand and learn."

Mack was feeling a combination of relief, excitement, and wonder. He never thought of himself in those terms. The combination of emotions was too much for him to bear. Mack let out an audible "Yeah!" to the nearly empty coffee shop. He began to chuckle, which grew into a full bout of laughter. "Yes!" he shouted again. Other patrons began to laugh at the visible joy. John sat with water in his eyes. The joy Mack was experiencing filled his heart. He had never experienced anything like this before; he felt full.

The owner of the coffee shop who had been watching Mack's reactions walked over and joked with the men. He delicately asked what the two had been discussing to get such a joyful response. After John and Mack had explained their journey, the owner thanked them for sharing. He began to recount the difference he was witnessing in Mack over the course of their visits to the coffee shop.

"What you are doing, please keep going. You aren't simply bringing purpose to your life, but you are impacting us as well. We feel your joy. You have become great additions to our regular family here. We are about to close for the night, but if you need to, please stay and finish your discussion. After I lock the door, I will be in the back cleaning and closing. Take as long as you need, but let me know when you leave."

"Thank you," Mack said as the smile remained from his breakthrough.

"Mack, I'm excited for you and your students. They are getting a connected, inspired teacher who is dedicated to their learning. You'll help them unlock their understanding and support them in applying it to new concepts. Your ability to empower them will pay dividends across God's universe for years to come and that's not an exaggeration. It's real."

"I'm beyond excited. This clarity is powerful. I have my purpose and I feel energized."

"You're ready for the last step in the process Mack. It is time for the E. Engage."

"OK, how do I do that?" Mack sat back wishing he could finish enjoying the earlier revelation.

"Engage is the easiest and most rewarding part of the process to start, but it is the most difficult to stay in. Engage is simply doing what you are meant to do. This is where the journey of R.I.S.E. takes off and you jump and fly. Remember, you may fall and get scratched and hurt along the way, but you will eventually soar."

"What do I need to do to engage, John?"

"You have already started with your focus on kindness and gratitude, but where you go from here has to come from within. Listen to God. He is always talking. Spend time in reflection and continue to recalibrate, inspire, seek your gifts and purpose in all you do, and do what you feel is necessary to make that happen. Remember who you are, Mack. Don't let distraction get you to take your eyes off your purpose and who you are. This is critical."

"John, why do I get the feeling that our Monday meetings are coming to a close?"

"Do you know the secret to awaken and rise? I mean, the real secret?" John stared directly into Mack's eyes.

"Uh, I'm not sure. Can you give me a hint?"

"There is no secret. This isn't something where you need a sage or expert to guide you. Once you have the formula and you know your purpose, it's critical that you are the one living it. I can't live it for you and I am not a holder of the information. I'm just the conduit that's available and willing to be used by God to share this message.

"This is His truth and one that will empower you to live far above the fray. It will take you to another level in life. However, now that I've shared this, I feel strongly that He is impressing on my heart to finish my book. I need to focus my time on putting the words down that He has for me to share. I'm not trying to be trite, but you are ready to RISE. I'm here if you need me and I hope that through our meetings we have become friends."

Mack looked blankly at John and drew a deep breath.

"We aren't friends, John. We are more. We are brothers." As Mack finished his sentence, his eyes welled up with tears. He stood and almost lunged across at John to give him a bear hug.

"Thank you, John. Thank you." Mack repeated this over and over. "I'm so sorry for how things started with us, but I couldn't be more grateful for how they've turned out."

"Yes, we're brothers, Mack. I'm grateful to be where we are now too. You know where to find me if you need me and please let's meet once I am done with the book. I want to stay in touch."

"Absolutely," uttered Mack while he wiped his eyes. "Let me know as soon as you are done. I want to read it."

John grinned, "You will be one of the first, my friend." His excitement about the journey was electrifying.

CHAPTER TWENTY-EIGHT
MORE TO COME

As John's book was coming into being, he was spending considerable time thinking and talking about RISE. He thought about how it changed his life and how it helped Mack. He was intentionally reflective in how it caused both of them to see their world differently. Denise and Grace continued to push John's understanding through their insights. Even though the application of RISE started as a one-time thing for John, he knew it was much more. It was a way to live life and stay in your purpose. It defeated disillusionment and reconnected individuals with their ability to make an impact. RISE empowers people to overcome difficulties and find greater joy. He began to see that RISE was a powerful part of everyday life.

"RISE is a continuing process, one that is needed when I start the day," he wrote in his journal.

RISE worked when dealing with trying situations at work; his children even used it to find their way through school and a variety of difficult situations.

"What I find most curious is that I don't ever RISE away from needing help, but when I do RISE, I get above the distractions that surround me. It is a way to focus on contributing to the greater good and to make a difference in the universe," he wrote. John paused and looked out the window of the coffee shop, he then wrote, "Through RISE, piece by piece, you are given peace."

John's book was quite the personal journey. He recounted his story and found himself writing about parts of his life he thought would have stayed locked up in personal secrecy. He was nervous to take the final step towards the book's completion. Fear began to rear its ugly head in an attempt to take hold of him. He came home from writing, sat down, and gazed out the window. Denise knew John wasn't admiring nature; she could feel something was amiss.

"Are you OK?" she asked.

"I don't know if I can do this. It's too personal. It's too raw. I'm nervous," John said sheepishly.

"John, you started this experience wanting to share love and hope. What you are experiencing now is the opposite. Fear is attempting to chase out your love and hope. You have too much in your heart to allow that to happen. Think about the message given to you. Recalibrate yourself, Inspire yourself, Seek your purpose, and Engage in it."

Denise put her hand on John's shoulder and then walked out of the room. He knew she was right. She returned with a letter and John recognized the return address immediately. It was from Mack. In a moment where he needed it most, God was speaking. John simply needed to be quiet and listen.

In the letter, Mack described what had taken place in his life since their last meeting. It was filled with positive change and hope. Mack told John about a student with whom he had connected who was turning his life around. He discussed how he shared RISE with his colleagues. Even though they were dealing with a leader who was destructive in words and deeds, they were able to overcome him by focusing on their purpose. "It has made us bullet-proof," Mack wrote. "We are so focused on doing what we are here to accomplish that we don't give any time or energy toward distraction."

Mack continued on to discuss the impact that the time they spent together in Kefi had on his family and friends. Mack had become a leader and an inspiration to those around him. His ripple effect was growing and people were being touched in amazing ways.

Finally, Mack ended his letter thanking John for being willing and available to share the message that was placed upon his heart.

Every day I am grateful that you opened up to me. Even when I hated you completely, you put it out there and loved me enough to share the message of Awaken and RISE. You were vulnerable to someone you couldn't trust and stepped to the edge of the cliff. I hope the book is coming along nicely and you are almost done. I know the world needs to hear what you have to share. Be a conduit and let God use you. Thank you, my brother.

Hoping to see you soon,
Mack

The letter was the most memorable of John's life.

"God is always talking to us. I just have to be quiet, pay attention, and listen," John said to himself. "I can do this."

In the days that followed, John finished *Awaken and Rise*. On faith, he submitted it to a variety of publishers and agents.

As if by divine design, John received multiple offers for the book. Going through the traditional publishing process is a much longer task than anyone can imagine. There were many ups and downs, but a year after completing the book, *Awaken and Rise* was sent to stores and outlets. John purchased copies for many friends and family members and of course, Mack. The feedback was positive and filled with love. John knew he had helped the people who read it and it gave him joy. He was engaged in his gifts and living in his purpose, but he didn't know what was happening across the universe. Six months after the initial publication, he received a call from his agent.

"John are you ready for this?"

"Sure," John responded.

"The publisher just called me and they have stacks of mail for you."

John was calm and he had no idea of what scope they were talking about.

"We'd like you to take a trip to the publisher to see this. How soon can you get on a plane?"

John was beginning to understand that this wasn't normal.

"I guess I can be on one Friday night."

"That's too far out. Can you get there by Wednesday?"

"Ok," John said, now becoming excited at the thought of what he was going to see.

When John arrived at the office, he was greeted with wide eyes and smiles. He was told they have never seen a response like this before as they led John into a large room. It was lined with stacks of boxes filled with letters. John's heart skipped a beat as he observed the response his book generated.

John began to read the letters and his heart filled. He heard from people all over the world. They shared their stories of how they broke the mold of their lives and how they found their gifts and purpose. Many letters shared how John's message reconnected them with the love and purpose that brought them to their chosen careers. The letters shared the differences people were making with others through their own ripple effect. John was overjoyed to know that people were finding their purpose. The disillusioned were finding connection and those who were once ruled by fear began to take courageous leaps to soar. John had spent three hours reading letter after letter when his agent walked into the room.

"So what do you think?" She smiled.

"This is amazing. To touch all of these lives makes it all worth it."

"There is one more thing you should know. Come into the conference room."

As the two of them walked down the hall into the conference room, John heard some discussion coming from a group of huddled people at the end of a long conference table. A collective hush fell upon them when they noticed John.

A woman at the head of the table cleared her throat.

"John are you interested in doing any speaking?"

"Absolutely! I have been doing some locally, but I feel drawn to a larger audience. In fact, I have some big ideas about it," he smiled as he finished.

"John, the box you see on the table, it's filled with requests for you to share your story of how people can make an impact. The invitations were from schools, businesses, communities, and organizations all over the world. Stunned, John picked up one of the letters.

"I'll do it," John said with great joy.

"Which one?" his agent asked.

"All of them. Every last one. If there is a conflict, let's try and figure something out. I'm here to help people and inspire them to live a life that they never thought was possible. My purpose is to do that. I cannot ignore it. If they are gracious enough to invite me, I'll do everything I can to be there."

The days, weeks, and months ahead were filled with hundreds of opportunities to share RISE. John immersed himself in his gift of speaking to inspire people to find connection and purpose. His talks were energizing and heartfelt, and despite his early fear, his vulnerability was the part that people were inspired by the most. In a world of showmanship, people need true inspiration and authentic purpose. Within a year of doing speaking engagements across the globe, John received a call from his agent about an upcoming event.

"The venue for next week's talk is too small and we have to move."

John felt a bit uneasy about the switch and he wondered if that would cause confusion for people to attend. He didn't see any other option and he reluctantly agreed.

In the days leading up to the event tickets were selling faster than ever. John spent time in reflection and he felt God was about to show him something special. As John took the stage, he looked out into the audience and he found himself looking at 100,000 faces who filled the stadium. Electricity shot through his body as he shared the message given to him. The hope, the love, the awaken, and the RISE.

He described how deep his sleep was and how God's universe conspired to wake him up. John shared how God used those around him to get above the distraction of life, how RISE impacted him, and how it could tremendously impact everyone who embraced it.

John closed the evening with two quotes he loved dearly. He looked out into the crowd and said, "To this day, I will never forget these things that I have learned. 'Our greatest glory is not in never falling, but in rising every time we fall.' No matter where you have been or what regrets you have, let them go. Find your story. Find your gifts. Find your purpose. Engage in it. RISE! Do it. Do it now in this moment. Don't look back, but remember the lessons of the past. You will make a difference. You will make an impact. Your path is unique, but it is yours to live and live with no regrets. Remember, 'it is all secretly perfect.' God bless you and thank you."

John's Famous SHERPA PLAYLIST

The Sherpa playlist was a vehicle of inspiration for John as he searched for what God and His universe had planned for him. Please enjoy the musical journey that aided in John's process to RISE.

You can also find a link to this playlist on www.brianlidle.com or by using the QR code or link listed at the bottom of the playlist.

1. Awake My Soul – Mumford and Sons
2. If I Ever Get Around to Living – John Mayer
3. Ocean – Live - John Butler
4. Under Pressure – David Bowie and Queen
5. Up All Night (Frankie Miller Goes to Hollywood) – Counting Crows
6. Come Together - Beatles
7. Secret Touch - Rush
8. Down Under 2012 - Solo Acoustic – Colin Hay
9. In Repair – John Mayer
10. Empire State of Mind (Part II) Broken Down - Alicia Keys
11. Gimme Shelter – The Rolling Stones
12. All I Really Want – Alanis Morissette
13. Vultures – John Mayer
14. Elvis Went to Hollywood – Counting Crows
15. Sweet Child O' Mine – Guns and Roses
16. Voodoo Child – Jimi Hendrix
17. Little Wing – Stevie Ray Vaughn
18. Sultans of Swing – Dire Straits
19. Do You Feel Like We Do – Peter Frampton
20. Vapor Trail – Rush
21. Uninvited – Alanis Morissette
22. Authority – Genevieve

23. Open Your Eyes – Snow Patrol
24. Blue Eyes – Cary Brothers
25. Thank U – Alanis Morissette
26. Freedom! '90 – George Michael
27. Let's Go Crazy - Prince
28. One Little Victory - Rush
29. Stranglehold – Ted Nugent
30. Far Cry – Rush
31. The Sound of Muzak – Porcupine Tree
32. Castles Made of Sand – Jimi Hendrix
33. What You Want – John Butler Trio
34. Yellow Ledbetter – Pearl Jam
35. Criminal – Fiona Apple
36. Clockwork Angels - Rush
37. All Along the Watchtower – Jimi Hendrix
38. The House Of The Rising Sun – The Animals
39. Where The Streets Have No Name – U2
40. Goodnight Elisabeth – Live at Heineken Music Hall – Counting Crows
41. My Brilliant Feat – Colin Hay
42. Hotel California - Eagles
43. Ghost Rider – Rush
44. Lay Your Hands On Me – Thompson Twins
45. F.U. – Pigeons Playing Ping Pong
46. Canned Heat – Jamiroquai
47. Are You Gonna Go My Way – Lenny Kravitz
48. Daniella – John Butler Trio
49. Cliffs Of Dover – Eric Johnson
50. Time After Time – Cyndi Lauper
51. I Still Haven't Found What I'm Looking For – U2
52. Zebra – Live – John Butler Trio
53. Always On The Run – Lenny Kravitz
54. Little L - Jamiroquai
55. Don't You (Forget About Me) – Simple Minds

56. Wonderwall – Oasis
57. La Villa Strangiato – Rush
58. I Want To Take You Higher – Sly & The Family Stone
59. Purple Rain – Prince
60. I Belong To You – Lenny Kravitz
61. Virtual Insanity – Jamiroquai
62. Seven Days in Sunny June – Jamiroquai
63. Hands Clean – Alanis Morissette
64. Message In A Bottle – The Police
65. Tom Sawyer – Rush
66. Stairway to Heaven – Led Zeppelin
67. The Spirit of Radio – Rush

TINYURL.COM/THESHERPA

Bibliography

Coehlo, P. (1998). The Alchemist. New York, NY: Harper Collins.

Curry, M. [marcuscurry]. (2016, January). Steve Harvey: You Have to Jump [Video file]. Retrieved from: https://www.youtube.com/watch?v=kILVFRIUtT8

Macedo, M. (2017). Be Yourself, Tell Your Story, Do Something That Matters (meganmacedo.com).

Pressfield, S. (2002). The War of Art: Break Through the Blocks and Win Your Inner Creative Battles. New York, NY: Black Irish Entertainment.

Robinson, Sir K. (2009). The Element: How Finding Your Passion Changes Everything. New York, NY: The Penguin Group.

ACKNOWLEDGEMENTS

Thank you to God for your Son and all of the blessings, trials, and steps along this journey.

My wife, Michele: thank you for being my everything.
My children: Chloe, Sophia, & Gavin thank you for being you.
My parents, Bob and Talli: thank you for your love and support.

My Kitchen Cabinet:
Mike McDonough, Kristin McDonough, Mark Tremayne, & Alicia Tremayne – Your loyalty, love, and support mean so much (FWAF). Thank you for always standing by me!
Lori Ludwig – Our conversations about faith and the universe were a catalyst for me. Thank you for all the love and support!
Sharon Esswein – My dear friend, you saw it before I would admit it. Thank you for teaching me and allowing God to use you to open my eyes to my possibilities!

My friends who supported me as beta readers and critical thinkers:
Art Gase
Jenna Hire
Kris Lucas
Amber Riley
Kelly Silwani
Brooke Wilming

Dr. Coyte Cooper – I am forever grateful for your encouragement and help. You are the real deal!

Jennifer Deese – Your ability to see and create what I feel never ceases to amaze me. Thank you for all you have done to make this a reality. I could not have done this without you. You are an amazing person and talent!

Mo, Hisham, and Fatma Muhidin – Your light spirit and generosity have taught me so much. Thank you for the hours of conversations and a wonderful space to write.

Jon Gordon, Paulo Coehlo, Steve Farber, Steven Pressfield, Megan Macedo, Brene Brown, Oprah Winfrey, John Butler, Colin Hay, Genevieve Schatz, Geddy Lee, Alex Lifeson, and Neil Peart – your work has served to inspire and connect with me in the dark and light times. Thank you for your contributions to my universe.

Thank you to the many who support me and this endeavor!

ABOUT THE AUTHOR

Brian Lidle is an author, educator, and speaker who believes in the power of our unique gifts and our ability to use those gifts for a greater purpose.

Brian had the privilege of growing up in Poland, Ohio, a suburb of Youngstown. It was here he learned the values of faith, family, loyalty, and hard work. Never one to avoid the chance to share a smile, Brian is known for his sense of humor and ability to connect with others.

Brian's formal education includes three years of Biblical Studies, an undergraduate degree in Education from Youngstown State University, and a Masters Degree in Educational Leadership from Ashland University. Along with his formal education, Brian has had the honor of learning from an outstanding group of coaches and educational leaders. His passions include music, spiritual understanding, deep conversations, and seeing people succeed by making their dreams a reality.

After spending years as a successful leader, educator, and coach, Brian had an awakening. He realized that our worth was not found in our successes or failures, but in how we impact the lives of those around us. He was revitalized by the truth that our legacy doesn't reflect our accomplishments, but reflects the person we are and the people we help.

Brian has dedicated himself to helping and inspiring people to embrace the greatness that resides within and to remain uncompromising in being the person we were designed to be through his website and writing. You can visit him at brianlidle.com where he has a blog and resources to help you - Awaken and Rise.

Brian currently resides in the Columbus, OH area with his amazing wife and their three vibrant children.

> *"The world doesn't need another copy. It needs you."*
> *- Brian Lidle*

Brian may be available to speak at your next event!

Please contact The Brian Lidle Company at

thebrianlidlecompany@gmail.com

and we will work to meet your needs.

WWW.BRIANLIDLE.COM

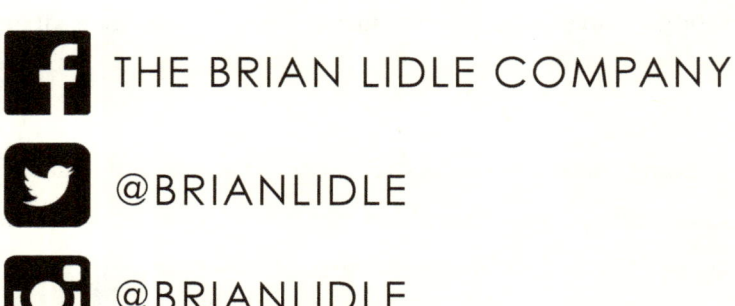

THE GUIDE TO
R.I.S.E.

After reading **Awaken and Rise**, you may find yourself wondering if there is something more. You may be wondering about your gifts and purpose.

The Guide to R.I.S.E. was created with you in mind. This guide takes you through a process similar to John's journey to find your gifts and purpose. This helpful process can be found at our website along with other content intended to inspire and motivate you to go for your dreams.

Find it at BrianLidle.com

"Our greatest glory is not in never falling, but in RISING every time we fall."

www.ingramcontent.com/pod-product-compliance
Lightning Source LLC
Chambersburg PA
CBHW032053090426
42744CB00005B/202